The UK Tefal Dual Zone AIR FRYER Cookbook with Pictures

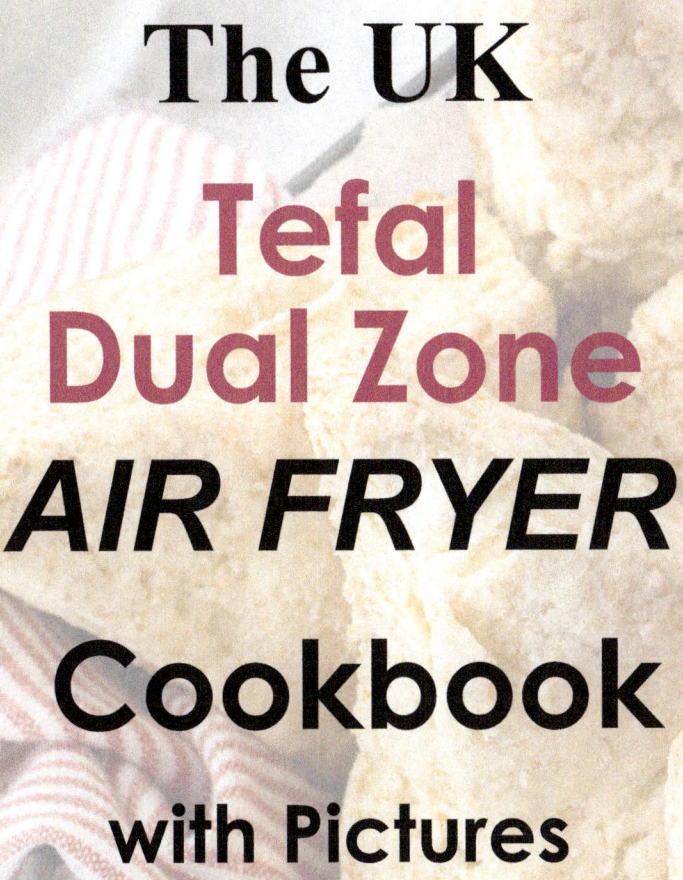

Delicious, Quick & No-Stress British Recipes for Tefal 2-Basket Air Fryer | Cook Main and Side Dish Synchronously

Leah Atkinson

Copyright © 2024 By Leah Atkinson
All rights reserved.

No part of this book may be reproduced, transmitted, or distributed in any form or by any means without permission in writing from the publisher except in the case of brief quotations embodied in critical articles or reviews.

Legal & Disclaimer

The content and information in this book is consistent and truthful, and it has been provided for informational, educational and business purposes only.

The illustrations in the book are from the website shutterstock.com, depositphoto.com and freepik.com and have been authorized.

The content and information contained in this book has been compiled from reliable sources, which are accurate based on the knowledge, belief, expertise and information of the Author. The author cannot be held liable for any omissions and/or errors.

Table of Content

INTRODUCTION 1
CHAPTER 1   MEET THE TEFAL DUAL ZONE AIR FRYER 2
CHAPTER 2   BREAKFAST 8
CHAPTER 3   POULTRY 14
CHAPTER 4   VEGETABLES 20
CHAPTER 5   FISH AND SEAFOOD 26
CHAPTER 6   LAMB 32
CHAPTER 7   BEEF 38
CHAPTER 8   PORK 44
CHAPTER 9   SNACK 50
CHAPTER 10 DESSERT 56

APPENDIX 1: TEFAL DUAL ZONE AIR FRYER TIMETABLE 62
APPENDIX 2: MEASUREMENT CONVERSION CHART 64
APPENDIX 3: RECIPES INDEX 65

INTRODUCTION

Hello there, food enthusiasts! I'm Leah Atkinson, and if there's one thing I absolutely adore, it's the joy of indulging in delicious meals. However, I found myself stuck in a culinary rut, spending too much time cooking and feeling bored with the same old recipes. That's when The UK Tefal Dual Zone Air Fryer burst into my life like a breath of fresh, flavourful air.

Let me tell you, this kitchen marvel has revolutionized my cooking game. Not only is its operation wonderfully simple, but its generous capacity allows me to cook up a storm without the hassle of constant monitoring. What truly sets The UK Tefal Dual Zone Air Fryer apart is its ability to cook two different foods simultaneously, catering to all my diverse cravings.

Imagine the delight of preparing a hearty main dish and a delectable side at the same time, effortlessly. That's the magic of this 8-in-1 air fryer. It's not just a kitchen appliance; it's a game-changer, reigniting the passion for creating mouthwatering dishes in the comfort of your home.

To share my newfound excitement and ease in the kitchen, I've curated a special recipe book dedicated to The UK Tefal Dual Zone Air Fryer. This collection is a treasure trove of simple and convenient recipes, perfect for both beginners and seasoned cooks. Each recipe comes with detailed operating steps, ensuring that everyone can unleash the full potential of this fantastic appliance.

If you're tired of the same old meals and want to rediscover the joy of cooking, then this recipe book is your culinary passport. Say goodbye to boredom in the kitchen, and hello to a world of delicious possibilities with The UK Tefal Dual Zone Air Fryer. Trust me; it's time to elevate your cooking experience. Join me on this flavourful journey, and let's make every meal an extraordinary delight!

CHAPTER 1

MEET THE TEFAL DUAL ZONE AIR FRYER

Advantages of Tefal Air Fryer ··· 3

Before First Use Guidelines ·· 4

How to Cook with Tefal Air Fryer? ·· 5

Useful Tips ··· 6

Cleaning and Storage ·· 6

The Tefal Easy Fry Dual Zone Digital Air Fryer introduces a new era of cooking convenience, seamlessly combining efficiency and versatility. Its standout feature is the dual-zone design, featuring two drawers (5.2L/3.1L) that cater to various meal sizes. Whether you're cooking for yourself or the entire family, the flexible drawers provide the perfect solution.

This air fryer doesn't just excel in speed, offering a remarkable 40% faster cooking time compared to traditional ovens, but also stands out in energy efficiency with up to 70% savings. Beyond the realm of air frying, the appliance boasts eight automatic programs, making roasting, baking, dehydrating, and more, a breeze. The intuitive design includes user-friendly controls with '1' and '2' buttons, ensuring straightforward operation.

With a commitment to healthier cooking, the Tefal Easy Fry Dual Zone Digital Air Fryer produces the same crispy texture with a staggering 99% less added fat than traditional deep frying methods. Its Sync Mode allows for dual cooking with precise timing, enabling the preparation of two distinct dishes simultaneously. As an all-in-one solution, this appliance eliminates the need for preheating, making cooking even more efficient. The Tefal Easy Fry Dual Zone Digital Air Fryer is a game-changer, promising a delightful culinary experience with every use.

Knowing the Control Panel

Get acquainted with the intuitive control panel of your Tefal Easy Fry Dual Zone Digital Air Fryer to maximize its cooking potential. Here's a detailed guide to help you navigate the functions effectively:

- **Drawer Activation:**
Use the '1' and '2' buttons to activate the corresponding drawers. '1' is designed for the larger 5.3L drawer, suitable for family-sized meals. '2' activates the smaller drawer, perfect for solo portions or smaller dishes.

- **Cooking Modes:**
Explore the diverse cooking modes available by using the dedicated buttons on the control panel. From Fries and Chicken to Vegetables, Fish, Dessert, Dehydrate, and Manual mode, each setting is crafted to cater to specific culinary requirements.

- **Manual Mode:**
Take control of the cooking process with Manual mode. Adjust the temperature using the '+' and '-' buttons within the range of 40-200°C. Fine-tune the cooking time by pressing the '+' and '-' buttons, providing flexibility for a tailored cooking experience.

- **Sync Mode:**
Activate Sync Mode when using both drawers to ensure precise timing for dual dishes. This feature is ideal for coordinating the cooking of two different foods simultaneously, ensuring both are ready to serve at the same time.

- **Start/Stop Button:**
The Start/Stop button is the command center, initiating and halting the cooking process. Press it to switch on the appliance and begin your culinary adventure. It also serves to stop cooking when your dishes are ready.

- **Temperature and Time Display:**
The digital display showcases the selected temperature and cooking time. Adjust these settings according to your recipe requirements for optimal results.

Understanding the Tefal Easy Fry Dual Zone Digital Air Fryer's control panel ensures that you have complete command over your cooking sessions. Experiment with the different modes and settings to unlock the appliance's versatility, enabling you to create a wide array of delicious, healthy meals effortlessly.

Advantages of Tefal Air Fryer

The Tefal Easy Fry Dual Zone Digital Air Fryer presents several advantages that elevate your cooking experience:

1. Dual-Zone Flexibility:

Benefit from two differently sized drawers (5.2L/3.1L), offering versatility for both individual meals and larger family portions.

2. Time and Energy Efficiency:

Enjoy 40% faster cooking compared to conventional ovens, saving valuable time in the kitchen.
Achieve up to 70% energy savings, contributing to an eco-friendly cooking approach.

3. Culinary Versatility:

Explore a multitude of cooking possibilities with 8 automatic programs, including roasting, baking, dehydrating, and more.
Eliminate guesswork and effortlessly diversify your menu with this all-in-one kitchen solution.

4. Healthier Cooking Options:

Indulge in guilt-free meals with 99% less added fat compared to traditional deep frying methods.
Prepare healthier versions of your favorite dishes, from crispy chips to succulent burgers.

5. Sync Mode for Dual Cooking:

Master the art of dual cooking with Sync Mode, allowing you to perfectly time the preparation of two distinct dishes.
Ideal for coordinating main courses and side dishes for a seamless dining experience.

6. Effortless Operation:

Experience hassle-free cooking with user-friendly controls, including '1' and '2' buttons for easy drawer activation.
The Extra Crisp air frying technology eliminates the need for preheating, streamlining the cooking process.

7. Intuitive Cleaning:

Simplify post-cooking cleanup with dishwasher-safe drawers and grids, ensuring a convenient and time-saving cleaning routine.

8. Eco-conscious Design:

Contribute to a greener kitchen with an appliance designed for energy efficiency, aligning with modern sustainability practices.

The Tefal Easy Fry Dual Zone Digital Air Fryer encapsulates these advantages, offering a comprehensive solution for efficient, versatile, and healthier cooking in the contemporary kitchen.

Before First Use Guidelines

Before embarking on your culinary journey with the Tefal Easy Fry Dual Zone Digital Air Fryer, it's essential to follow these pre-use guidelines for optimal performance and safety:

1. Unboxing and Setup:

Carefully remove all packaging material from the appliance, ensuring you discard any plastic or protective covers.
Pay attention to stickers on the appliance, excluding the QR code sticker. Remove any stickers that may interfere with the cooking process.

2. Thorough Cleaning:

Prior to the first use, thoroughly clean both drawers and removable grids with hot water, a small amount of washing-up liquid, and a non-abrasive sponge. These components are dishwasher safe, allowing for easy and convenient cleaning after each use.

3. Wipe Down the Appliance:

Use a damp cloth to wipe both the interior and exterior of the appliance. This step is crucial as the appliance generates hot air during operation, and cleanliness ensures optimal performance.

4. Precautions for Hot Air Operation:

As the appliance operates by producing hot air, it is crucial not to fill the drawers with oil or frying fat, which could compromise its effectiveness.

5. Placement and Ventilation:

Position the appliance on a flat, stable, and heat-resistant surface, away from water splashes.

To prevent overheating, avoid placing the air fryer in a corner or below a wall cupboard. Allow a minimum gap of 15cm around the appliance for proper air circulation.

6. Switching On:

Press the Start/Stop button to switch on the appliance.
By default, the Fries mode is displayed for drawer 1 while OFF is displayed for drawer 2. Choose the desired drawer by pressing '1' or '2' buttons.

7. Selection and Cancellation:

To select a drawer, press the corresponding '1' or '2' button. To cancel the selection, press the same button again.
Never exceed the maximum amount indicated in the cooking guide, as this could impact the quality of the cooking results.

Following these pre-use guidelines ensures that your Tefal Easy Fry Dual Zone Digital Air Fryer is primed for safe and efficient operation, setting the stage for delightful culinary experiences.

How to Cook with Tefal Air Fryer?

Unlock the full potential of your Tefal Easy Fry Dual Zone Digital Air Fryer with these comprehensive steps for both solo meals and family feasts.

Cooking with 1 Drawer (Drawer 1 or 2):

- When preparing a single portion or snack, choose either '1' or '2' to activate the corresponding drawer. The smaller 3.1L drawer ('2') is ideal for single portions or snacks, while the larger 5.3L drawer ('1') caters to family-sized meals, accommodating even a 1.4 kg whole chicken.

- Select your preferred cooking mode, such as Fries, Chicken, Vegetables, or others, using the dedicated buttons.
- Adjust the temperature and cooking time to your liking with the intuitive controls. The digital display ensures easy monitoring of the cooking progress.
- Press the Start/Stop button to initiate the cooking process. Once done, open the designated drawer to reveal your perfectly cooked dish, tailored to your portion needs.

Cooking with 2 Drawers in Sync:

- For a more elaborate meal with dual components, activate both drawers by pressing '1' and '2'. This initiates Sync Mode, ensuring precise timing for cooking two different dishes simultaneously.
- Select the cooking modes for each drawer based on your culinary requirements. Adjust temperatures and times independently for each drawer using the controls.
- Once settings are configured, press the Start/Stop button to commence the cooking process. The air fryer handles the synchronization, ensuring both components are ready to serve at the same time.
- Retrieve your culinary creations, each perfectly cooked in its own drawer. Sync Mode streamlines the process, making it effortless to coordinate a cohesive and delicious multi-dish meal.

Experiment with the versatile cooking modes, temperatures, and times to tailor your Tefal Easy Fry Dual Zone Digital Air Fryer to a variety of recipes. From quick solo meals to synchronized feasts, this appliance offers a delightful and efficient cooking experience.

Useful Tips

Enhance your culinary mastery with the Tefal Easy Fry Dual Zone Digital Air Fryer using these insightful tips:

√ **Adjust Cooking Times for Size:**
Recognize that smaller foods generally require a slightly shorter cooking time than their larger counterparts. Tailor your cooking times accordingly for optimal results.

√ **Shake Smaller Foods Midway:**
Improve the end result and prevent uneven cooking by shaking smaller-sized foods halfway through the cooking time. This ensures even crisping and a delightful texture.

√ **Crispy Potatoes with a Twist:**
Elevate your potato game by achieving extra crispiness. Before cooking, add a small amount of oil and shake to evenly cover. A recommended 14ml of oil can transform your potatoes into a crispy delight.

√ **Versatile Snacking:**
Discover the versatility of your air fryer. Snacks that can be traditionally cooked in an oven can also be prepared with ease in this appliance. Experiment with various snacks to broaden your culinary horizons.

√ **Optimal Fries Quantity:**
Achieve the perfect batch of fries by following the recommended quantity. Aim for 1,200 grams, distributing 800 grams in drawer 1 and 400 grams in drawer 2. This ensures even cooking and consistent crispiness.

√ **Quick and Easy Pastries:**
Expedite snack preparation by using ready-made puff and shortcrust pastry. Create filled snacks effortlessly, adding a touch of convenience to your culinary creations.

√ **Baking and Frying Delicacies:**
Enhance your baking or frying experience by placing an oven dish in the appliance's bowl. Ideal for cakes, quiches, or delicate filled ingredients, choose from materials like silicon, stainless steel, aluminium, or terracotta for a customized cooking experience.

√ **Efficient Food Reheating:**
Utilize your air fryer for reheating food efficiently. Set the temperature to 160°C for up to 10 minutes. Adjust the cooking time based on food quantity, ensuring thorough reheating.

Incorporate these tips into your cooking routine to unleash the full potential of your Tefal Easy Fry Dual Zone Digital Air Fryer and elevate your culinary creations.

Cleaning and Storage

Maintain the peak performance of your Tefal Easy Fry Dual Zone Digital Air Fryer by following these cleaning and storage guidelines:

Cleaning:

Post-Use Routine:
After each use, it's essential to clean the appliance promptly to ensure optimal hygiene and performance.

Non-Stick Bowl and Grid:
The bowl and grid feature a non-stick coating. Avoid using metal kitchen utensils or abrasive cleaning materials, as these may damage the nonstick coating.

Cooling Down:
Before cleaning, remove the mains plug from the wall socket and allow the appliance to cool down. For a faster cooling process, remove the bowl.

Exterior Cleaning:
Wipe the exterior of the appliance with a damp cloth to remove any surface dirt.

Bowl and Grid Cleaning:
Clean the bowl and grid with hot water, mild washing-up liquid, and a non-abrasive sponge. For stubborn residues, a degreasing liquid can be used.

Dishwasher Compatibility:
Note that the bowl and grid are dishwasher safe for added convenience. Simply place them in the dishwasher for a thorough cleaning.

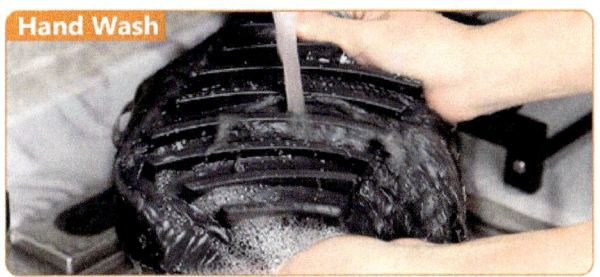

Tip for Stubborn Debris:
If there's food debris or residue stuck at the bottom of the bowl and grid, fill them with hot water and some washing-up liquid. Let them soak for approximately 10 minutes before rinsing them clean and allowing them to dry.

Interior Cleaning:
Wipe the inside of the appliance with hot water and a damp cloth to remove any remaining traces of food or grease.

Heating Element:
Use a dry, cleaning brush to clean the heating element, removing any food residues that may have accumulated during cooking.

Avoid Immersion:
Do not immerse the entire appliance in water or any other liquid to prevent damage.

Storage:

Unplugging and Cooling Down:
Before storing the appliance, ensure it is unplugged from the power source and has completely cooled down.

Clean and Dry Parts:
Ensure all parts of the air fryer are clean and thoroughly dry before storage. This helps prevent any potential issues and ensures a hygienic cooking environment for the next use.

Following these cleaning and storage practices will help you maintain your Tefal Easy Fry Dual Zone Digital Air Fryer in top-notch condition for delicious and hassle-free cooking experiences.

CHAPTER 2
BREAKFAST

Quick Blueberry Muffins ·· 9

Cornflakes Toast Sticks ·· 9

Tasty Coffee Doughnuts ·· 10

Gold Avocado Fries ·· 10

Nutty Apple Muffins ··· 11

Feta Mushroom Frittata ··· 11

Pitta and Pepperoni Pizza ·· 12

Mustard Pork Meatballs ·· 12

Kale and Potato Nuggets ··· 12

Classic British Breakfast ·· 13

Sourdough Croutons ·· 13

Feta Spinach Omelette ·· 13

Quick Blueberry Muffins

🕒 PREP TIME: 10 MINUTES, COOK TIME: 15 MINUTES, MAKES 8 MUFFINS

- 80 ml rapeseed oil
- 1 egg
- 160 g flour
- 120 ml milk
- 100 g blueberries, fresh or frozen and thawed
- 100 g sugar
- 10 g baking powder
- ¼ tsp. salt

1. In a medium bowl, stir together flour, sugar, baking powder, and salt.
2. In a separate bowl, combine the rapeseed oil, egg, and milk and mix well.
3. Add the egg mixture to dry ingredients and stir just until moistened.
4. Gently stir in the blueberries.
5. Spoon the batter evenly into parchment-paper-lined muffin cups.
6. Install the grids in drawers. Place 5 muffin cups on the drawer 1 and 3 muffin cups on the drawer 2, then insert the drawers in unit.
7. Press Start/Stop button, select Zone 1, select Dessert setting, set temperature to 160°C, and set time to 15 minutes. Select Zone 2 and repeat the settings for Zone 1. Press Start/Stop button to begin cooking, until tops spring back when touched lightly.
8. When cooking is complete, let the muffins cool slightly and serve warm.

Cornflakes Toast Sticks

🕒 PREP TIME: 10 MINUTES, COOK TIME: 8 MINUTES, SERVES 4

- Cooking spray
- 6 slices sandwich bread, each slice cut into 4 strips
- 2 eggs
- 120 ml milk
- 80 g crushed cornflakes
- ½ tsp. pure vanilla extract
- ⅛ tsp. salt
- Maple syrup, for dipping

1. In a small bowl, beat together the eggs, milk, salt, and vanilla.
2. Put the crushed cornflakes on a plate or in a shallow dish.
3. Dip the bread strips in egg mixture, shake off excess, and roll in cornflake crumbs.
4. Spray both sides of bread strips with cooking spray.
5. Install the grids in drawers. According to the size of the drawers, arrange the bread strips on the drawers reasonably. Insert the drawers in unit.
6. Press Start/Stop button, select Zone 1, select Manual setting, set temperature to 200°C, and set time to 8 minutes. Select Zone 2 and repeat the settings for Zone 1. Press Start/Stop button to begin cooking.
7. Flip the bread strips for even cooking and browning halfway through cooking.
8. When cooking is complete, transfer the bread strips to a plate. Serve warm with maple syrup.

Chapter 2: BREAKFAST / 9

Gold Avocado Fries

PREP TIME: 5 MINUTES, COOK TIME: 8 MINUTES, SERVES 4

- 2 large avocados, sliced
- 2 eggs, beaten
- 100 g breadcrumbs
- 60 g wholemeal flour
- ¼ tsp. paprika
- Salt and ground black pepper, to taste

1. Sprinkle the paprika, salt and pepper on the slices of avocado.
2. Lightly coat the avocados with flour. Dredge them in the eggs, before covering with breadcrumbs.
3. Install the large grid in drawer 1. Place the avocado slices on the drawer, then insert the drawer in unit.
4. Press Start/Stop button, select Zone 1, select Fries setting, set temperature to 200°C, and set time to 8 minutes. Press Start/Stop button to begin cooking.
5. Shake the avocado fries for even cooking and browning halfway through cooking.
6. When cooking is complete, transfer the avocado fries to a plate. Serve warm.

Tasty Coffee Doughnuts

PREP TIME: 5 MINUTES, COOK TIME: 8 MINUTES, SERVES 6

- 15 ml sunflower oil
- 50 g sugar
- 120 g flour
- 60 ml coffee
- 5 g baking powder
- 1 tbsp. aquafaba
- ½ tsp. salt

1. In a large bowl, combine the sugar, flour, salt, and baking powder.
2. Add the coffee, aquafaba, and sunflower oil and mix until a dough is formed. Leave the dough to rest in and the refrigerator.
3. Remove the dough from the fridge and divide up, kneading each section into a doughnut.
4. Install the grids in drawers. According to the size of the drawers, arrange the doughnuts in a single layer on the drawers reasonably. Insert the drawers in unit.
5. Press Start/Stop button, select Zone 1, select Dessert setting, set temperature to 200°C, and set time to 8 minutes. Select Zone 2 and repeat the settings for Zone 1. Press Start/Stop button to begin cooking.
6. When cooking is complete, transfer the doughnuts to a plate. Serve warm.

Nutty Apple Muffins

PREP TIME: 15 MINUTES, COOK TIME: 12 MINUTES, MAKES 8 MUFFINS

- 40 g melted butter
- 1 egg
- 180 g unsweetened apple sauce
- 120 g flour
- 70 g sugar
- 40 g pancake syrup
- 30 g chopped walnuts
- 30 g diced apple
- 5 g baking powder
- 1 g baking soda
- ¼ tsp. salt
- 2 g cinnamon
- ¼ tsp. ginger
- ¼ tsp. nutmeg
- ½ tsp. vanilla extract

1. In a large bowl, stir together the flour, sugar, baking powder, baking soda, cinnamon, ginger, nutmeg and salt.
2. In a small bowl, beat the egg until frothy. Add the syrup, butter, apple sauce, and vanilla and mix well.
3. Pour the egg mixture into dry ingredients and stir just until moistened.
4. Gently stir in nuts and diced apple.
5. Divide the batter among 8 parchment-paper-lined muffin cups.
6. Install the grids in drawers. Place 5 muffin cups on the drawer 1 and 3 muffin cups on the drawer 2, then insert the drawers in unit.
7. Press Start/Stop button, select Zone 1, select Dessert setting, set temperature to 160°C, and set time to 12 minutes. Select Zone 2 and repeat the settings for Zone 1. Press Start/Stop button to begin cooking, until toothpick inserted in centre comes out clean.
8. When cooking is complete, serve warm.

Feta Mushroom Frittata

PREP TIME: 15 MINUTES, COOK TIME: 17 MINUTES, SERVES 2

- Cooking spray, as required
- 15 ml olive oil
- 300 g button mushrooms, sliced thinly
- 3 eggs
- 45 g feta cheese, crumbled
- ½ red onion, sliced thinly
- Salt, to taste

1. Grease two 10 cm ramekins lightly with cooking spray.
2. Heat the olive oil on medium heat in a frying pan and add the onion and mushrooms.
3. Sauté for about 5 minutes and transfer the mushroom mixture into a bowl.
4. Whisk together eggs and salt in a small bowl and transfer into the prepared ramekins.
5. Put the mushroom mixture over the eggs and top with feta cheese.
6. Install the grids in drawers. Place one ramekin on each drawer. Insert the drawers in unit.
7. Press Start/Stop button, select Zone 1, select Dessert setting, set temperature to 160°C, and set time to 12 minutes. Select Zone 2 and repeat the settings for Zone 1. Press Start/Stop button to begin cooking.
8. When cooking is complete, let the ramekins cool slightly and serve warm.

Chapter 2: BREAKFAST / 11

Pitta and Pepperoni Pizza

PREP TIME: 10 MINUTES, COOK TIME: 8 MINUTES, SERVES 1

- 5 ml olive oil
- 1 pitta bread
- 6 pepperoni slices
- 25 g grated Mozzarella cheese
- 15 ml pizza sauce
- ¼ tsp. garlic powder
- ¼ tsp. dried oregano

1. Spread the pizza sauce on top of the pitta bread. Put the pepperoni slices over the sauce, followed by the cheese.
2. Season with garlic powder and oregano.
3. Install the large grid in drawer 1 and grease with olive oil. Place the pitta pizza on the drawer, then insert the drawer in unit.
4. Press Start/Stop button, select Zone 1, select Manual setting, set temperature to 180°C, and set time to 8 minutes. Press Start/Stop button to begin cooking.
5. When cooking is complete, serve warm.

Mustard Pork Meatballs

PREP TIME: 15 MINUTES, COOK TIME: 15 MINUTES, SERVES 4

- 225 g minced pork
- 1 onion, chopped
- 8 g fresh basil, chopped
- 5 g cheddar cheese, grated
- 5 g Parmesan cheese, grated
- 5 ml honey
- 1 tsp. garlic paste
- 1 tsp. mustard
- Salt and black pepper, to taste

1. Mix together all the ingredients in a bowl until well combined.
2. Make small equal-sized meatballs from the mixture.
3. Install the large grid in drawer 1. Place the meatballs on the drawer, then insert the drawer in unit.
4. Press Start/Stop button, select Zone 1, select Manual setting, set temperature to 200°C, and set time to 15 minutes. Press Start/Stop button to begin cooking.
5. Shake the meatballs for even cooking and browning halfway through cooking.
6. When cooking is complete, transfer the meatballs to a plate. Serve warm.

Kale and Potato Nuggets

PREP TIME: 10 MINUTES, COOK TIME: 18 MINUTES, SERVES 4

- Cooking spray
- 5 ml extra virgin olive oil
- 400 g potatoes, boiled and mashed
- 300 g kale, rinsed and chopped
- 30 ml milk
- 1 clove garlic, minced
- Salt and ground black pepper, to taste

1. In a frying pan over medium heat, sauté the garlic in the olive oil, until it turns golden brown. Sauté with the kale for another 3 minutes and remove from the heat.
2. Mix the mashed potatoes, kale and garlic in a bowl. Pour in the milk and sprinkle with salt and pepper.
3. Shape the potato mixture into nuggets and spritz with cooking spray.
4. Install the large grid in drawer 1. Place the nuggets on the drawer, then insert the drawer in unit.
5. Press Start/Stop button, select Zone 1, select Manual setting, set temperature to 200°C, and set time to 15 minutes. Press Start/Stop button to begin cooking.
6. With 7 minutes remaining, press Start/Stop to pause the unit. Remove the drawer from unit and flip the nuggets over. Reinsert drawer in unit and press Start/Stop to resume cooking.
7. When cooking is complete, transfer the nuggets to a plate. Serve warm.

Classic British Breakfast

PREP TIME: 5 MINUTES, COOK TIME: 20 MINUTES, SERVES 2

- **240 g potatoes, sliced and diced**
- **400 g baked beans**
- **2 eggs**
- **15 ml olive oil**
- **1 sausage**
- **Salt, to taste**

1. Break the eggs onto a 18 x 13-cm baking dish and sprinkle with salt.
2. Lay the baked beans on the dish, next to the eggs.
3. In a bowl, coat the diced potatoes with the olive oil. Sprinkle with salt.
4. Install the grids in drawers. Place the baking dish on the drawer 1 and potato slices on the drawer 2, then insert the drawers in unit.
5. Press Start/Stop button, select Zone 1, select Manual setting, set temperature to 190°C, and set time to 16 minutes. Select Zone 2, select Vegetables setting, set temperature to 200°C, and set time to 20 minutes. Press SYNC and Start/Stop button to begin cooking.
6. With 5 minutes remaining, press Start/Stop to pause the unit. Remove the drawers from unit. Slice up the sausage and throw the slices on top of the beans and egg. Shake the potatoes for 10 seconds. Reinsert drawers in unit and press Start/Stop to resume cooking.
7. When cooking is complete, serve immediately.

Sourdough Croutons

PREP TIME: 5 MINUTES, COOK TIME: 6 MINUTES,, SERVES 2

- **15 ml olive oil**
- **300 g cubed sourdough bread, 2.5 cm cubes**
- **1 tsp. fresh thyme leaves**
- **¼ tsp. salt**
- **Freshly ground black pepper, to taste**

1. Combine all the ingredients in a large bowl.
2. Install the large grid in drawer 1. Place the bread cubes on the drawer, then insert the drawer in unit.
3. Press Start/Stop button, select Zone 1, select Manual setting, set temperature to 200°C, and set time to 6 minutes. Press Start/Stop button to begin cooking.
4. Shake the bread cubes for even cooking and browning halfway through cooking.
5. When cooking is complete, transfer the bread cubes to a plate. Serve warm.

Feta Spinach Omelette

PREP TIME: 10 MINUTES, COOK TIME: 10 MINUTES, SERVES 1

- **5 ml olive oil**
- **3 eggs**
- **15 g ricotta cheese**
- **30 g chopped spinach**
- **3 g chopped parsley**
- **Salt and ground black pepper, to taste**

1. Grease a 18 x13 cm baking dish with olive oil.
2. In a bowl, beat the eggs with a fork and sprinkle salt and pepper.
3. Add the ricotta cheese, spinach, and parsley. Transfer the spinach mixture into the baking dish.
4. Install the large grid in drawer 1. Place the baking dish on the drawer, then insert the drawer in unit.
5. Press Start/Stop button, select Zone 1, select Dessert setting, set temperature to 160°C, and set time to 10 minutes. Press Start/Stop button to begin cooking, until the egg is set.
6. When cooking is complete, serve warm.

CHAPTER 3
POULTRY

Roasted Chicken with Potatoes 15

Bacon Wrapped Chicken Breasts 15

Asian Turkey Meatballs 16

Glazed Chicken Wings 16

Chinese Chicken Drumsticks 17

Sweet and Sour Chicken Thighs 17

Crunchy Chicken Wings 18

Juicy Chicken Drumsticks 18

Chicken with Veggies 18

Mouthwatering Turkey Roll 19

Flavoury Chicken Kebabs 19

Roasted Chicken Breasts with Broccoli 19

Roasted Chicken with Potatoes

PREP TIME: 15 MINUTES, COOK TIME: 45 MINUTES, SERVES 2

- 15 ml olive oil
- 1.4 kg whole chicken
- 225 g small potatoes
- Salt and black pepper, as required

1. Season the whole chicken and potatoes with salt and black pepper and drizzle lightly with olive oil.
2. Install the grids in drawers. Place the chicken on the drawer 1 and potatoes on the drawer 2, then insert the drawers in unit.
3. Press Start/Stop button, select Zone 1, select Chicken setting, set temperature to 200°C, and set time to 45 minutes. Select Zone 2, select Vegetables setting, set temperature to 200°C, and set time to 30 minutes. Press SYNC and Start/Stop button to begin cooking.
4. With 20 minutes remaining, press Start/Stop to pause the unit. Remove the drawers from unit. Flip the chicken over and shake the potatoes for 10 seconds. Reinsert drawers in unit and press Start/Stop to resume cooking.
5. When cooking is complete, serve the chicken with potatoes.

Bacon Wrapped Chicken Breasts

PREP TIME: 20 MINUTES, COOK TIME: 28 MINUTES, SERVES 4

- 2 (225 g) chicken breasts, cut each breast in half horizontally
- 12 rashers of bacon
- 6-7 fresh basil leaves
- 30 ml water
- 30 ml fish sauce
- 15 g palm sugar
- 7 ml honey
- Salt and ground black pepper, as required

1. Cook the palm sugar in a small heavy-bottomed pan over medium-low heat for about 3 minutes until caramelised.
2. Stir in the basil, fish sauce and water and dish out in a small bowl.
3. Season each chicken breast with salt and black pepper and coat evenly with the palm sugar mixture.
4. Refrigerate to marinate for 6 hours and wrap each chicken piece with 3 rashers of bacon. Dip into the honey.
5. Install the large grid in drawer 1. Place the chicken breasts on the drawer, then insert the drawer in unit.
6. Press Start/Stop button, select Zone 1, select Chicken setting, set temperature to 200°C, and set time to 25 minutes. Press Start/Stop button to begin cooking.
7. Flip the chicken breasts for even cooking and browning halfway through cooking.
8. When cooking is complete, transfer the chicken breasts to a plate. Serve warm.

Chapter 3: POULTRY / 15

Glazed Chicken Wings

PREP TIME: 10 MINUTES, COOK TIME: 25 MINUTES, SERVES 4

- 8 chicken wings
- 15 g plain flour
- 15 ml fresh lemon juice
- 15 ml soy sauce
- 1 tsp. garlic, chopped finely
- ½ tsp. dried oregano, crushed
- Salt and freshly ground black pepper, to taste

1. Mix all the ingredients except the chicken wings in a large bowl.
2. Coat the wings generously with the marinade and refrigerate for about 2 hours.
3. Remove the chicken wings from marinade and sprinkle with flour evenly.
4. Install the large grid in drawer 1. Place the wings on the drawer, then insert the drawer in unit.
5. Press Start/Stop button, select Zone 1, select Chicken setting, set temperature to 200°C, and set time to 25 minutes. Press Start/Stop button to begin cooking.
6. Flip the wings for even cooking and browning halfway through cooking.
7. When cooking is complete, transfer the wings to a plate. Serve hot.

Asian Turkey Meatballs

PREP TIME: 10 MINUTES, COOK TIME: 13-14 MINUTES, SERVES 4

- 30 ml peanut oil, divided
- 450 g minced turkey
- 1 egg, beaten
- 1 small onion, minced
- 30 ml low-sodium soy sauce
- 30 g panko bread crumbs
- 30 g water chestnuts, finely chopped
- ½ tsp. ground ginger

1. In a frying pan, heat 15 ml peanut oil until hot. Add the onion and cook for about 1 to 2 minutes or until crisp and tender. Transfer the onion to a medium bowl.
2. Place the water chestnuts, ground ginger, soy sauce, and bread crumbs to the onion and mix well. Add the egg and stir well. Mix in the minced turkey until combined.
3. Form the turkey mixture into 2.5-cm meatballs. Drizzle the remaining 15 ml oil over the meatballs.
4. Install the grids in drawers. According to the size of the drawers, arrange the meatballs on the drawers reasonably. Insert the drawers in unit.
5. Press Start/Stop button, select Zone 1, select Chicken setting, set temperature to 190°C, and set time to 12 minutes. Select Zone 2 and repeat the settings for Zone 1. Press Start/Stop button to begin cooking.
6. Shake the meatballs for even cooking and browning halfway through cooking.
7. When cooking is complete, transfer the meatballs to a plate. Rest for 5 minutes before serving.

Chapter 3: POULTRY

Chinese Chicken Drumsticks

PREP TIME: 15 MINUTES, COOK TIME: 22 MINUTES, SERVES 4

- 3 ml sesame oil
- 4 (170 g) chicken drumsticks
- 15 ml oyster sauce
- 5 ml light soy sauce
- 1 tsp. Chinese five spice powder
- Salt and white pepper, as required

1. Mix the sesame oil, sauces, five spice powder, salt, and black pepper in a bowl.
2. Rub the chicken drumsticks with marinade and refrigerate for 40 minutes.
3. Install the large grid in drawer 1. Place the drumsticks on the drawer, then insert the drawer in unit.
4. Press Start/Stop button, select Zone 1, select Chicken setting, set temperature to 200°C, and set time to 22 minutes. Press Start/Stop button to begin cooking.
5. Flip the drumsticks for even cooking and browning halfway through cooking.
6. When cooking is complete, transfer the drumsticks to a plate. Serve warm.

Sweet and Sour Chicken Thighs

PREP TIME: 15 MINUTES, COOK TIME: 20 MINUTES, SERVES 2

- 2 (115 g) skinless, boneless chicken thighs
- 50 g corn flour
- 1 spring onion, finely chopped
- 1 garlic clove, minced
- 7 ml rice vinegar
- 7 ml soy sauce
- 5 g sugar
- Salt and black pepper, as required

1. Mix all the ingredients except the chicken thighs and corn flour in a bowl.
2. Place the corn flour in another bowl.
3. Coat the chicken thighs into the marinade and then dredge into the corn flour.
4. Install the large grid in drawer 1. Place the chicken thighs on the drawer, skin side down, then insert the drawer in unit.
5. Press Start/Stop button, select Zone 1, select Chicken setting, set temperature to 200°C, and set time to 20 minutes. Press Start/Stop button to begin cooking.
6. Flip the chicken thighs for even cooking and browning halfway through cooking.
7. When cooking is complete, transfer the chicken thighs to a plate. Serve warm.

Chapter 3: POULTRY / 17

Crunchy Chicken Wings

PREP TIME: 20 MINUTES, COOK TIME: 28 MINUTES, SERVES 2

- 500 g chicken wings, rinsed and trimmed
- 2 lemongrass stalk (white portion), minced
- 1 onion, finely chopped
- 50 g cornflour
- 15 ml soy sauce
- 22 ml honey
- Salt and white pepper, as required

1. Mix the lemongrass, chopped onion, soy sauce, honey, salt, and white pepper in a bowl.
2. Coat the chicken wings generously with marinade and refrigerate, covered to marinate overnight.
3. Install the large grid in drawer 1. Place the wings on the drawer, then insert the drawer in unit.
4. Press Start/Stop button, select Zone 1, select Chicken setting, set temperature to 200°C, and set time to 28 minutes. Press Start/Stop button to begin cooking.
5. Flip the wings for even cooking and browning halfway through cooking.
6. When cooking is complete, transfer the wings to a plate. Serve warm.

Juicy Chicken Drumsticks

PREP TIME: 10 MINUTES, COOK TIME: 22 MINUTES, SERVES 4

- 30 ml olive oil
- 4 boneless chicken drumsticks
- 60 ml Dijon mustard
- 1 g fresh rosemary, minced
- 2 g fresh thyme, minced
- 15 ml honey
- Salt and freshly ground black pepper, to taste

1. Mix all the ingredients in a bowl except the drumsticks until well combined.
2. Stir in the chicken drumsticks and coat generously with the mixture.
3. Cover and refrigerate to marinate overnight.
4. Install the large grid in drawer 1. Place the chicken drumsticks on the drawer, then insert the drawer in unit.
5. Press Start/Stop button, select Zone 1, select Chicken setting, set temperature to 200°C, and set time to 22 minutes. Press Start/Stop button to begin cooking.
6. Flip the drumsticks for even cooking and browning halfway through cooking.
7. When cooking is complete, transfer the drumsticks to a plate. Serve warm.

Chicken with Veggies

PREP TIME: 20 MINUTES, COOK TIME: 28 MINUTES, SERVES 2

- 30 ml olive oil
- 2 skinless, boneless chicken breasts
- 4 small artichoke hearts, quartered
- 4 fresh large button mushrooms, quartered
- ½ small onion, cut in large chunks
- 6 g fresh parsley, chopped
- 2 garlic cloves, minced
- 30 ml chicken broth
- 30 ml red wine vinegar
- 15 ml Dijon mustard
- ⅛ tsp. dried thyme
- ⅛ tsp. dried basil
- Salt and black pepper, as required

1. Mix the garlic, broth, vinegar, olive oil, mustard, thyme, and basil in a bowl.
2. Combine the artichokes, mushrooms, onions, salt, and black pepper in another bowl.
3. Install the grids in drawers. Place chicken breasts on the drawer 1 and and spread evenly with half of the mustard mixture. Arrange vegetables on the drawer 2, then insert the drawers in unit.
4. Press Start/Stop button, select Zone 1, select Chicken setting, set temperature to 190°C, and set time to 28 minutes. Select Zone 2, select Vegetables setting, set temperature to 200°C, and set time to 18 minutes. Press SYNC and Start/Stop button to begin cooking.
5. With 10 minutes remaining, press Start/Stop to pause the unit. Remove the drawers from unit. Coat the chicken breasts with the remaining mustard mixture and flip the side. Shake the vegetables for 10 seconds. Reinsert drawers in unit and press Start/Stop to resume cooking.
6. When cooking is complete, transfer the chicken and vegetables to a plate. Serve garnished with parsley.

Mouthwatering Turkey Roll

PREP TIME: 20 MINUTES, COOK TIME: 40 MINUTES, SERVES 4

- 30 ml olive oil
- 450 g turkey breast fillet, deep slit cut lengthwise with knife
- 1 small red onion, chopped finely
- 1 garlic clove, crushed
- 8 g fresh parsley, chopped finely
- 1½ tsps. ground cumin
- 1 tsp. ground cinnamon
- ½ tsp. red chilli powder
- Salt, to taste

1. Mix the onion, garlic, parsley, spices and olive oil in a small bowl.
2. Coat the open side of fillet with onion mixture and roll the fillet tightly.
3. Coat the outer side of roll with remaining spice mixture.
4. Install the large grid in drawer 1. Place the turkey breast on the drawer, then insert the drawer in unit.
5. Press Start/Stop button, select Zone 1, select Chicken setting, set temperature to 200°C, and set time to 20 minutes. Press Start/Stop button to begin cooking.
6. Flip the turkey breast for even cooking and browning halfway through cooking.
7. When cooking is complete, transfer the turkey breast to a plate. Serve warm.

Flavoury Chicken Kebabs

PREP TIME: 20 MINUTES, COOK TIME: 15 MINUTES, SERVES 3

- 450 g chicken tenders
- 4 spring onions, chopped
- 8 g sesame seeds, toasted
- 60 ml sesame oil
- 120 ml pineapple juice
- 120 ml soy sauce
- 6 g fresh ginger, finely grated
- 4 garlic cloves, minced
- A pinch of black pepper
- Wooden skewers, pres oaked

1. Mix the spring onions, ginger, garlic, pineapple juice, soy sauce, sesame oil, sesame seeds, and black pepper in a large baking dish.
2. Thread the chicken tenders onto pre-soaked wooden skewers.
3. Coat the skewers generously with marinade and refrigerate for 2 hours.
4. Install the grids in drawers. According to the size of the drawers, arrange the skewers in a single layer on the drawers reasonably. Insert the drawers in unit.
5. Press Start/Stop button, select Zone 1, select Chicken setting, set temperature to 190°C, and set time to 15 minutes. Select Zone 2 and repeat the settings for Zone 1. Press Start/Stop button to begin cooking.
6. Shake the skewers for even cooking and browning halfway through cooking.
7. When cooking is complete, transfer skewers to a plate. Serve warm.

Roasted Chicken Breasts with Broccoli

PREP TIME: 20 MINUTES, COOK TIME: 20 MINUTES, SERVES 3

- 20 g butter
- 450 g boneless, skinless chicken breasts, sliced
- 180 g small broccoli florets
- 1½ tbsps. dried parsley, crushed
- ½ tbsp. onion powder
- ½ tbsp. garlic powder
- ¼ tsp. red chilli powder
- ¼ tsp. paprika

1. Mix the butter, parsley and spices in a bowl.
2. Coat the sliced chicken and broccoli generously with the spice mixture.
3. Install the grids in drawers. Place the marinated chicken slices on the drawer 1 and broccoli on the drawer 2, then insert the drawers in unit.
4. Press Start/Stop button, select Zone 1, select Chicken setting, set temperature to 190°C, and set time to 20 minutes. Select Zone 2, select Vegetables setting, set temperature to 200°C, and set time to 15 minutes. Press SYNC and Start/Stop button to begin cooking.
5. With 8 minutes remaining, press Start/Stop to pause the unit. Remove the drawers from unit and shake for 10 seconds. Reinsert drawers in unit and press Start/Stop to resume cooking.
6. When cooking is complete, serve the chicken slices with broccoli.

CHAPTER 4
Vegetables

Mini Red Pepper Cups 21

Classic Hasselback Potatoes 21

Green Beans and Mushroom 22

Caramelised Brussels Sprouts 22

Roasted Asparagus with Grated Parmesan 23

Glazed Carrots 23

Broccoli with Cauliflower 24

Dehydrated Aubergine Slices 24

Roasted Mushrooms 24

Cheese Stuffed Mushrooms 25

Spices Stuffed Aubergines 25

Buttered Green Beans 25

Mini Red Pepper Cups

PREP TIME: 10 MINUTES, COOK TIME: 15 MINUTES, SERVES 4

- 7 ml olive oil
- 8 mini red bell peppers, tops and seeds removed
- 90 g feta cheese, crumbled
- 1 g fresh parsley, chopped
- Freshly ground black pepper, to taste

1. Mix the feta cheese, parsley, olive oil and black pepper in a bowl.
2. Stuff the red bell peppers with feta cheese mixture.
3. Install the grids in drawers. Place 5 peppers on the drawer 1 and 3 peppers on the drawer 2, then insert the drawers in unit.
4. Press Start/Stop button, select Zone 1, select Vegetables setting, set temperature to 200°C, and set time to 15 minutes. Select Zone 2 and repeat the settings for Zone 1. Press Start/Stop button to begin cooking.
5. When cooking is complete, transfer the peppers to a plate. Serve warm.

Classic Hasselback Potatoes

PREP TIME: 20 MINUTES, COOK TIME: 30 MINUTES, SERVES 4

- 30 ml olive oil
- 4 potatoes
- 16 g Parmesan cheese, shredded
- 3 g fresh chives, chopped

1. Cut slits along each potato about 0.5 cm apart with a sharp knife, making sure slices should stay connected at the bottom.
2. Install the large grid in drawer 1. Coat the potatoes with olive oil and arrange on the drawer, then insert the drawer in unit.
3. Press Start/Stop button, select Zone 1, select Vegetables setting, set temperature to 200°C, and set time to 30 minutes. Press Start/Stop button to begin cooking.
4. When cooking is complete, transfer the potatoes to a plate. Top with chives and Parmesan cheese to serve.

Chapter 4: VEGETABLES / 21

Caramelised Brussels Sprouts

PREP TIME: 10 MINUTES, COOK TIME: 20 MINUTES, SERVES 4

- 20 g butter, melted
- 600 g Brussels sprouts, trimmed and halved
- Salt and black pepper, to taste

1. Mix all the ingredients in a bowl and toss to coat well.
2. Install the large grid in drawer 1. Place the Brussels sprouts on the drawer, then insert the drawer in unit.
3. Press Start/Stop button, select Zone 1, select Vegetables setting, set temperature to 200°C, and set time to 20 minutes. Press Start/Stop button to begin cooking.
4. Shake the Brussels sprouts for even cooking and browning half-way through cooking.
5. When cooking is complete, transfer Brussels sprouts to a plate. Serve warm.

Green Beans and Mushroom

PREP TIME: 15 MINUTES, COOK TIME: 15 MINUTES, SERVES 6

- 45 ml olive oil
- 700 g fresh green beans, trimmed
- 200 g fresh button mushrooms, sliced
- 40 g French fried onions
- 30 ml fresh lemon juice
- 1 tsp. ground sage
- 1 tsp. garlic powder
- 1 tsp. onion powder
- Salt and black pepper, to taste

1. Mix the green beans, mushrooms, oil, lemon juice, sage, and spices in a bowl and toss to coat well.
2. Install the grids in drawers. Place green beans on the drawer 1 and mushrooms on the drawer 2, then insert the drawers in unit.
3. Press Start/Stop button, select Zone 1, select Vegetables setting, set temperature to 200°C, and set time to 15 minutes. Select Zone 2, select Vegetables setting, set temperature to 200°C, and set time to 12 minutes. Press SYNC and Start/Stop button to begin cooking.
4. With 6 minutes remaining, press Start/Stop to pause the unit. Remove the drawers from unit and shake for 10 seconds. Reinsert drawers in unit and press Start/Stop to resume cooking.
5. When cooking is complete, serve green beans with mushrooms.

Roasted Asparagus with Grated Parmesan

PREP TIME: 15 MINUTES, COOK TIME: 20 MINUTES, SERVES 3

- 15 g butter, melted
- 450 g fresh asparagus, trimmed
- 15 g Parmesan cheese, grated
- 1 tsp. garlic powder
- Salt and black pepper, to taste

1. Mix the asparagus, Parmesan cheese, butter, garlic powder, salt, and black pepper in a bowl and toss to coat well.
2. Install the large grid in drawer 1. Place the asparagus on the drawer, then insert the drawer in unit.
3. Press Start/Stop button, select Zone 1, select Vegetables setting, set temperature to 200°C, and set time to 20 minutes. Press Start/Stop button to begin cooking.
4. Flip the asparagus for even cooking and browning halfway through cooking.
5. When cooking is complete, transfer the asparagus to a plate. Serve warm.

Glazed Carrots

PREP TIME: 10 MINUTES, COOK TIME: 16 MINUTES, SERVES 4

- 15 ml olive oil
- 500 g carrots, peeled and cut into large chunks
- 15 ml honey
- Salt and black pepper, to taste

1. Mix all the ingredients in a bowl and toss to coat well.
2. Install the large grid in drawer 1. Place the carrots on the drawer, then insert the drawer in unit.
3. Press Start/Stop button, select Zone 1, select Vegetables setting, set temperature to 200°C, and set time to 16 minutes. Press Start/Stop button to begin cooking.
4. Flip the carrots for even cooking and browning halfway through cooking.
5. When cooking is complete, transfer carrots to a plate. Serve warm.

Chapter 4: VEGETABLES

Broccoli with Cauliflower

PREP TIME: 15 MINUTES, COOK TIME: 20 MINUTES, SERVES 4

- 200 g broccoli, cut into 2.5 cm pieces
- 200 g cauliflower, cut into 2.5 cm pieces
- 15 ml olive oil
- Salt, as required

1. Mix the vegetables, olive oil, and salt in a bowl and toss to coat well.
2. Install the grids in drawers. Place broccoli on the drawer 1 and cauliflower on the drawer 2, then insert the drawers in unit.
3. Press Start/Stop button, select Zone 1, select Vegetables setting, set temperature to 200°C, and set time to 14 minutes. Select Zone 2, select Vegetables setting, set temperature to 200°C, and set time to 20 minutes. Press SYNC and Start/Stop button to begin cooking.
4. With 8 minutes remaining, press Start/Stop to pause the unit. Remove the drawers from unit and shake for 10 seconds. Reinsert drawers in unit and press Start/Stop to resume cooking.
5. When cooking is complete, serve immediately.

Dehydrated Aubergine Slices

PREP TIME: 15 MINUTES, COOK TIME: 6 HOURS, SERVES:4

- 400 g aubergines, washed and peeled

1. Blanch the entire aubergine in a large pot of boiling water for 15 seconds or less, then transfer it to a large bowl of ice water until cool. Cut the aubergine into 3-mm slices.
2. Install the grids in drawers. According to the size of the drawers, arrange the aubergine slices on the drawers reasonably. Insert the drawers in unit.
3. Press Start/Stop button, select Zone 1, select Dehydrate setting, set temperature to 40°C, and set time to 6 hours. Select Zone 2 and repeat the settings for Zone 1. Press Start/Stop button to begin cooking.
4. When cooking is complete, transfer the aubergine slices to a plate. Serve immediately.

Roasted Mushrooms

PREP TIME: 10 MINUTES, COOK TIME: 22 MINUTES, SERVES 4

- 15 g butter, melted
- 900 g mushrooms, quartered
- 30 ml white vermouth
- 2 g herbs de Provence
- ½ tsp. garlic powder

1. Mix herbs de Provence, garlic powder and butter and mushrooms in a large bowl.
2. Install the grids in drawers. Place 600 g mushrooms on the drawer 1 and the remaining 300 g on the drawer 2, then insert the drawers in unit.
3. Press Start/Stop button, select Zone 1, select Vegetables setting, set temperature to 200°C, and set time to 22 minutes. Select Zone 2 and repeat the settings for Zone 1. Press Start/Stop button to begin cooking.
4. With 5 minutes remaining, press Start/Stop to pause the unit. Remove the drawers from unit and stir the mushrooms with white vermouth. Reinsert drawers in unit and press Start/Stop to resume cooking.
5. When cooking is complete, transfer the mushrooms to a plate. Serve warm.

Cheese Stuffed Mushrooms

PREP TIME: 10 MINUTES, COOK TIME: 7 MINUTES, SERVES 4

- 30 ml olive oil
- 200 g button mushrooms, stemmed
- 20 g cheddar cheese, grated
- 20 g mozzarella cheese, grated
- 12 g Italian dried mixed herbs
- 1 tsp. dried dill
- Salt and freshly ground black pepper, to taste

1. Mix the mushrooms, Italian dried mixed herbs, oil, salt and black pepper in a bowl and toss to coat well.
2. Install the large grid in drawer 1. Place the mushrooms on the drawer and top with mozzarella cheese and cheddar cheese, then insert the drawer in unit.
3. Press Start/Stop button, select Zone 1, select Vegetables setting, set temperature to 200°C, and set time to 7 minutes. Press Start/Stop button to begin cooking.
4. When cooking is complete, transfer the mushrooms to a plate and sprinkle with dried dill to serve.

Spices Stuffed Aubergines

PREP TIME: 15 MINUTES, COOK TIME: 15 MINUTES, SERVES 4

- 20 ml olive oil, divided
- 8 baby aubergines
- ¾ tbsp. dry mango powder
- ¾ tbsp. ground coriander
- 1 g ground turmeric
- 1 g ground cumin
- 1 g garlic powder
- Salt, to taste

1. Make 2 slits from the bottom of each aubergine leaving the stems intact.
2. Add 5 ml olive oil, mango powder, coriander, cumin, turmeric and garlic powder in a bowl, combine well.
3. Fill each slit of aubergines with this spices mixture. Brush the outer side of each aubergine with remaining olive oil.
4. Install the grids in drawers. Place 5 aubergines on the drawer 1 and 3 aubergines on the drawer 2, then insert the drawers in unit.
5. Press Start/Stop button, select Zone 1, select Vegetables setting, set temperature to 190°C, and set time to 15 minutes. Select Zone 2 and repeat the settings for Zone 1. Press Start/Stop button to begin cooking.
6. When cooking is complete, transfer the aubergines to a plate. Serve warm.

Buttered Green Beans

PREP TIME: 10 MINUTES, COOK TIME: 12 MINUTES, SERVES 4

- cooking spray
- 5 g butter, melted
- 500 g green beans, washed and trimmed
- 15 ml fresh lemon juice
- ¼ tsp. garlic powder
- Salt and freshly ground pepper, to taste

1. Put all the ingredients in a large bowl and combine well.
2. Install the large grid in drawer 1. Place the green beans on the drawer, then insert the drawer in unit.
3. Press Start/Stop button, select Zone 1, select Vegetables setting, set temperature to 200°C, and set time to 12 minutes. Press Start/Stop button to begin cooking.
4. Flip the green beans for even cooking and browning halfway through cooking.
5. When cooking is complete, transfer the green beans to a plate. Serve warm.

CHAPTER 5
Fish and Seafood

Buttered Scallops ·· 27

Crispy Flounder with Green Beans ·· 27

Garlic Prawns ··· 28

Sweet and Sour Glazed Cod ··· 28

Cod with Asparagus ··· 29

Lemon Tilapia ·· 29

Cajun Salmon ·· 30

Paprika Prawns and Brussels Sprouts ·· 30

Simple Salmon Bites ·· 30

Chilli Cod Cakes ··· 31

Panko Halibut Strips ·· 31

Herbed Haddock with Cheese Sauce ··· 31

Buttered Scallops

⏱ PREP TIME: 10 MINUTES, COOK TIME: 8 MINUTES, SERVES 2

- 15 g butter, melted
- 300 g sea scallops
- ½ tbsp. fresh thyme, minced
- Salt and black pepper, to taste

1. Mix all the ingredients in a large bowl and toss to coat well.
2. Install the large grid in drawer 1. Place the scallops on the drawer, then insert the drawer in unit.
3. Press Start/Stop button, select Zone 1, select Fish setting, set temperature to 200°C, and set time to 8 minutes. Press Start/Stop button to begin cooking.
4. Flip the scallops for even cooking and browning halfway through cooking.
5. When cooking is complete, transfer the scallops to a plate. Serve warm.

Crispy Flounder with Green Beans

⏱ PREP TIME: 15 MINUTES, COOK TIME: 15 MINUTES, SERVES 3

- 60 ml vegetable oil
- 3 (170 g) flounder fillets
- 1 egg
- 100 g dry breadcrumbs
- 1 lemon, sliced
- 5 ml sesame oil
- 225 g fresh green beans, trimmed and cut in half
- 15 ml soy sauce

1. Whisk the egg in a shallow bowl and mix the breadcrumbs and vegetable oil in another bowl.
2. Dip the flounder fillets into the whisked egg and coat with the breadcrumb mixture.
3. Mix the green beans, soy sauce, and sesame oil in a bowl and toss to coat well.
4. Install the grids in drawers. Place the flounder fillets on the drawer 1 and green beans on the drawer 2, then insert the drawers in unit.
5. Press Start/Stop button, select Zone 1, select Fish setting, set temperature to 200°C, and set time to 15 minutes. Select Zone 2, select Vegetables setting, set temperature to 200°C, and set time to 12 minutes. Press SYNC and Start/Stop button to begin cooking.
6. When cooking is complete, serve the flounder fillets and green beans with lemon slices.

Chapter 5: FISH AND SEAFOOD / 27

Sweet and Sour Glazed Cod

PREP TIME: 20 MINUTES, COOK TIME: 12 MINUTES, SERVES 2

- 5 ml water
- 4 (100 g) cod fillets
- 80 ml honey
- 80 ml soy sauce
- 15 ml rice wine vinegar

1. Mix the soy sauce, honey, vinegar and water in a small bowl.
2. Reserve about half of the mixture in another bowl.
3. Stir the cod fillets in the remaining mixture until well coated.
4. Cover and refrigerate to marinate for 3 hours.
5. Install the large grid in drawer 1. Place the cod fillets on the drawer, then insert the drawer in unit.
6. Press Start/Stop button, select Zone 1, select Fish setting, set temperature to 200°C, and set time to 12 minutes. Press Start/Stop button to begin cooking.
7. Flip the fish for even cooking and browning halfway through cooking.
8. When cooking is complete, transfer the cod fillets to a plate. Coat with the reserved marinade and serve hot.

Garlic Prawns

PREP TIME: 15 MINUTES, COOK TIME: 8 MINUTES, SERVES 2

- 15 ml olive oil
- 350 g medium prawns, peeled and deveined
- 20 ml fresh lemon juice
- 1 tsp. lemon pepper
- ¼ tsp. paprika
- ¼ tsp. garlic powder

1. Mix the olive oil, lemon juice, lemon pepper, paprika and garlic powder in a large bowl.
2. Stir in the prawns and toss until well combined.
3. Install the large grid in drawer 1. Place the prawns on the drawer, then insert the drawer in unit.
4. Press Start/Stop button, select Zone 1, select Fish setting, set temperature to 200°C, and set time to 8 minutes. Press Start/Stop button to begin cooking.
5. Flip the prawns for even cooking and browning halfway through cooking.
6. When cooking is complete, transfer the prawns to a plate. Serve warm.

Cod with Asparagus

PREP TIME: 15 MINUTES, COOK TIME: 20 MINUTES, SERVES 2

- 2 (170 g) boneless cod fillets
- 6 g fresh parsley, roughly chopped
- 6 g fresh dill, roughly chopped
- 1 bunch asparagus
- 15 ml olive oil
- 22 ml fresh lemon juice
- 1 tsp. dried basil
- Salt and black pepper, to taste

1. Mix the olive oil, lemon juice, dill, basil, parsley, salt, and black pepper in a small bowl.
2. Combine the cod and ¾ of the olive oil mixture in another bowl.
3. Coat the asparagus with the remaining oil mixture.
4. Install the grids in drawers. Place cod on the drawer 1 and asparagus on the drawer 2, then insert the drawers in unit.
5. Press Start/Stop button, select Zone 1, select Fish setting, set temperature to 200°C, and set time to 15 minutes. Select Zone 2, select Vegetables setting, set temperature to 200°C, and set time to 20 minutes. Press SYNC and Start/Stop button to begin cooking.
6. With 8 minutes remaining, press Start/Stop to pause the unit. Remove the drawers from unit. Flip the cod and shake the asparagus for 10 seconds. Reinsert drawers in unit and press Start/Stop to resume cooking.
7. When cooking is complete, serve the cod immediately with asparagus.

Lemon Tilapia

PREP TIME: 5 MINUTES, COOK TIME: 12 MINUTES, SERVES 4

- 15 ml olive oil
- 4 (150 g) tilapia fillets
- 15 ml lemon juice
- 1 tsp. minced garlic
- ½ tsp. chilli powder

1. In a large, shallow bowl, mix together the lemon juice, olive oil, garlic, and chilli powder to make a marinade. Place the tilapia fillets in the bowl and coat evenly.
2. Install the large grid in drawer 1. Place tilapia fillets in a single layer on the drawer, then insert the drawer in unit.
3. Press Start/Stop button, select Zone 1, select Fish setting, set temperature to 200°C, and set time to 12 minutes. Press Start/Stop button to begin cooking, until the fish is cooked and flakes easily with a fork.
4. When cooking is complete, transfer the tilapia fillets to a plate. Serve warm.

Chapter 5: FISH AND SEAFOOD / 29

Cajun Salmon

PREP TIME: 10 MINUTES, COOK TIME: 12 MINUTES, SERVES 2

- 2 (200 g) (2-cm thick) salmon fillets
- 15 ml fresh lemon juice
- 1 tbsp. Cajun seasoning
- 2 g coconut sugar

- 2 (200 g) (2-cm thick) salmon fillets
- 15 ml fresh lemon juice
- 1 tbsp. Cajun seasoning
- 2 g coconut sugar

1. Season the salmon fillets evenly with Cajun seasoning and coconut sugar.
2. Install the large grid in drawer 1. Place the salmon on the drawer, then insert the drawer in unit.
3. Press Start/Stop button, select Zone 1, select Fish setting, set temperature to 200°C, and set time to 12 minutes. Press Start/Stop button to begin cooking.
4. When cooking is complete, transfer the salmon fillets to a plate. Drizzle with the lemon juice and serve hot.

Paprika Prawns and Brussels Sprouts

PREP TIME: 10 MINUTES, COOK TIME: 20 MINUTES, SERVES 2

- 45 ml olive oil, divided
- 500 g tiger prawns
- 400 g Brussels sprouts, trimmed and halved
- 30 g whole wheat breadcrumbs
- 30 g Parmesan cheese, shredded
- 15 ml balsamic vinegar
- ½ tsp. smoked paprika
- Salt and black pepper, to taste

1. Mix the prawns, 30 ml olive oil, paprika and salt to taste in a large bowl until well combined.
2. Combine the Brussels sprouts, vinegar, the remaining 15 ml oil, salt, and black pepper in another bowl and toss to coat well.
3. Install the grids in drawers. Place prawns on the drawer 1 and Brussels sprouts on the drawer 2, then insert the drawers in unit.
4. Press Start/Stop button, select Zone 1, select Fish setting, set temperature to 200°C, and set time to 12 minutes. Select Zone 2, select Vegetables setting, set temperature to 200°C, and set time to 20 minutes. Press SYNC and Start/Stop button to begin cooking.
5. With 8 minutes remaining, press Start/Stop to pause the unit. Remove the drawers from unit and shake for 10 seconds. Reinsert drawers in unit and press Start/Stop to resume cooking.
6. When cooking is complete, serve prawns with Brussels sprouts.

Simple Salmon Bites

PREP TIME: 15 MINUTES, COOK TIME: 15 MINUTES, SERVES 4

- Cooking spray
- 4 (140 g) tins pink salmon, skinless, boneless in water, drained
- 2 eggs, beaten
- 100 g whole-wheat panko bread crumbs
- 60 g finely minced red bell pepper
- 2 tbsps. parsley flakes
- 2 tsps. Old Bay seasoning

1. In a medium bowl, mix the salmon, eggs, red bell pepper, panko bread crumbs, parsley flakes, and Old Bay seasoning.
2. Using a small cookie scoop, form the salmon mixture into 20 balls.
3. Install the grids in drawers. According to the size of the drawers, arrange the balls on the drawers reasonably. Spray lightly with cooking spray. Insert the drawers in unit.
4. Press Start/Stop button, select Zone 1, select Fish setting, set temperature to 200°C, and set time to 15 minutes. Select Zone 2 and repeat the settings for Zone 1. Press Start/Stop button to begin cooking.
5. Shake the balls for even cooking and browning halfway through cooking.
6. When cooking is complete, transfer the salmon bites to a plate. Serve warm.

Chapter 5: FISH AND SEAFOOD

Chilli Cod Cakes

PREP TIME: 20 MINUTES, COOK TIME: 12 MINUTES, SERVES 6

- **500 g cod fillet**
- **1 egg**
- **80 g coconut, grated and divided**
- **15 ml fresh lime juice**
- **1 spring onion, finely chopped**
- **6 g fresh parsley, chopped**
- **1 tsp. fresh lime zest, finely grated**
- **1 tsp. red chilli paste**
- **Salt, as required**

1. Put the cod fillet, egg, lime zest, chilli paste, salt and lime juice in a food processor and pulse until smooth.
2. Transfer the cod mixture into a bowl and add spring onion, parsley and 2 tbsps. coconut.
3. Mix until well combined and make 12 equal-sized round cakes from the mixture.
4. Place the remaining coconut in a shallow bowl and coat the cod cakes with coconut.
5. Install the grids in drawers. Place 8 cakes on the drawer 1 and 4 cakes on the drawer 2, then insert the drawers in unit.
6. Press Start/Stop button, select Zone 1, select Fish setting, set temperature to 200°C, and set time to 12 minutes. Select Zone 2 and repeat the settings for Zone 1. Press Start/Stop button to begin cooking.
7. When cooking is complete, transfer the cod cakes to a plate. Serve warm.

Panko Halibut Strips

PREP TIME: 20 MINUTES, COOK TIME: 12 MINUTES, SERVES 2

- **2 eggs**
- **300 g skinless halibut fillets, cut into 2.5 cm strips**
- **150 g plain panko breadcrumbs**
- **4 tbsps. taco seasoning mix**
- **15 ml water**

1. Put the taco seasoning mix in a shallow bowl and whisk together the eggs and water in a second bowl.
2. Place the breadcrumbs in a third bowl.
3. Dredge the halibut with taco seasoning mix, then dip into the egg mixture and finally, coat evenly with the breadcrumbs.
4. Install the large grid in drawer 1. Place the halibut strips in a single layer on the drawer, then insert the drawer in unit.
5. Press Start/Stop button, select Zone 1, select Fish setting, set temperature to 200°C, and set time to 12 minutes. Press Start/Stop button to begin cooking.
6. Flip the strips for even cooking and browning halfway through cooking.
7. When cooking is complete, transfer the halibut strips to a plate. Serve warm.

(Note: Taco seasoning mix - Mix chilli powder, garlic powder, onion powder, red pepper flakes, oregano, paprika, cumin, salt and pepper in a small bowl. Store in an airtight container.)

Herbed Haddock with Cheese Sauce

PREP TIME: 10 MINUTES, COOK TIME: 12 MINUTES, SERVES 2

- **120 ml extra-virgin olive oil**
- **2 (170 g) haddock fillets**
- **20 g pine nuts**
- **10 g Parmesan cheese, grated**
- **12 g fresh basil, chopped**
- **Salt and black pepper, to taste**

1. Coat the haddock fillets evenly with olive oil and season with salt and black pepper.
2. Install the large grid in drawer 1. Place the haddock fillets on the drawer, then insert the drawer in unit.
3. Press Start/Stop button, select Zone 1, select Fish setting, set temperature to 200°C, and set time to 12 minutes. Press Start/Stop button to begin cooking.
4. Flip the haddock for even cooking and browning halfway through cooking.
5. Meanwhile, put the remaining ingredients in a food processor and pulse until smooth.
6. When cooking is complete, transfer the haddock fillets to a plate. Top the cheese sauce over the haddock fillets and serve hot.

CHAPTER 6
Lamb

Lamb Meatballs with Tomato Sauce ··· 33

Fantastic Lamb Leg ·· 33

Greek Lamb Rack ·· 34

Lamb with Potatoes ··· 34

Simple Lamb Chops ·· 35

Pesto Coated Rack of Lamb ·· 35

Italian Lamb Chops with Avocado Mayo ··· 36

Lamb Burger ··· 36

Fast Lamb Satay ·· 36

Lollipop Lamb Chops ·· 37

Scrumptious Lamb Chops ··· 37

Za'atar Lamb Loin Chops ··· 37

Lamb Meatballs with Tomato Sauce

PREP TIME: 20 MINUTES, COOK TIME: 27 MINUTES, SERVES 4

- For the Meatballs:
- 450 g minced lamb
- ½ small onion, finely diced
- 30 ml milk
- 1 egg yolk
- 5 g fresh parsley, finely chopped (plus more for garnish)
- 2 tsps. fresh oregano, finely chopped
- 1 clove garlic, minced
- Salt and freshly ground black pepper, to taste
- 60 g crumbled feta cheese, for garnish

- For the Tomato Sauce:
- 30 g butter
- 1 (800 g) tin crushed tomatoes
- 1 clove garlic, smashed
- Pinch crushed red pepper flakes
- ¼ tsp. ground cinnamon
- Salt, to taste
- Cooking spray

1. Combine all the ingredients for the meatballs in a large bowl and mix just until everything is combined. Shape the lamb mixture into 4-cm balls or shape the meat between two spoons to make quenelles.
2. Start the quick tomato sauce. Put the butter, garlic and red pepper flakes in a frying pan and heat over medium heat on the hob. Let the garlic sizzle a little, but before the butter browns, add the cinnamon and tomatoes. Bring to a simmer and simmer for 15 minutes. Season with salt.
3. Install the grids in drawers. According to the size of the drawers, arrange the meatballs on the drawers reasonably. Insert the drawers in unit.
4. Press Start/Stop button, select Zone 1, select Manual setting, set temperature to 200°C, and set time to 12 minutes. Select Zone 2 and repeat the settings for Zone 1. Press Start/Stop button to begin cooking.
5. With 6 minutes remaining, press Start/Stop to pause the unit. Remove the drawers from unit and flip the meatballs over. Reinsert drawers in unit and press Start/Stop to resume cooking.
6. When cooking is complete, transfer meatballs to a plate. To serve, spoon a pool of the tomato sauce onto plates and add the meatballs. Sprinkle the feta cheese on top and garnish with more fresh parsley. Serve immediately.

Fantastic Lamb Leg

PREP TIME: 10 MINUTES, COOK TIME: 50 MINUTES, SERVES 4

- 30 ml olive oil
- 900 g lamb leg
- 2 fresh rosemary sprigs
- 2 fresh thyme sprigs
- Salt and black pepper, to taste

1. Sprinkle the lamb leg with olive oil, salt and black pepper and wrap with herb sprigs.
2. Install the large grid in drawer 1. Place the lamb leg on the drawer, then insert the drawer in unit.
3. Press Start/Stop button, select Zone 1, select Manual setting, set temperature to 200°C, and set time to 50 minutes. Press Start/Stop button to begin cooking.
4. With 25 minutes remaining, press Start/Stop to pause the unit. Remove the drawer from unit and flip the lamb leg over. Reinsert drawer in unit and press Start/Stop to resume cooking.
5. When cooking is complete, transfer the lamb leg to a plate. Serve warm.

Chapter 6: LAMB / 33

Lamb with Potatoes

PREP TIME: 20 MINUTES, COOK TIME: 30 MINUTES, SERVES 2

- 5 ml olive oil
- 225 g lamb meat
- 2 small potatoes, peeled and halved
- ½ small onion, peeled and halved
- 1 garlic clove, crushed
- ½ tbsp. dried rosemary, crushed

1. Rub the lamb evenly with garlic and rosemary.
2. Add the potatoes in a large bowl and stir in the olive oil and onions.
3. Install the grids in drawers. Place lamb on the drawer 1 and vegetables on the drawer 2, then insert the drawers in unit.
4. Press Start/Stop button, select Zone 1, select Manual setting, set temperature to 190°C, and set time to 25 minutes. Select Zone 2, select Vegetables setting, set temperature to 200°C, and set time to 30 minutes. Press SYNC and Start/Stop button to begin cooking.
5. With 15 minutes remaining, press Start/Stop to pause the unit. Remove the drawers from unit and flip the lamb and vegetables over. Reinsert drawers in unit and press Start/Stop to resume cooking.
6. When cooking is complete, serve lamb with vegetables.

Greek Lamb Rack

PREP TIME: 5 MINUTES, COOK TIME: 14 MINUTES, SERVES 4

- 30-60 ml olive oil
- 1 lamb rib rack (7 to 8 ribs)
- 60 ml freshly squeezed lemon juice
- 25 g minced garlic
- 1 tsp. oregano
- 2 tsps. minced fresh rosemary
- 1 tsp. minced fresh thyme
- Salt and freshly ground black pepper, to taste

1. In a small mixing bowl, combine the lemon juice, oregano, rosemary, thyme, garlic, salt, black pepper, and olive oil and mix well.
2. Rub the herb mixture over the lamb, covering all the meat.
3. Install the large grid in drawer 1. Place the rack of lamb on the drawer, then insert the drawer in unit.
4. Press Start/Stop button, select Zone 1, select Manual setting, set temperature to 200°C, and set time to 14 minutes. Press Start/Stop button to begin cooking.
5. With 7 minutes remaining, press Start/Stop to pause the unit. Remove the drawer from unit and flip the rack of lamb over. Reinsert drawer in unit and press Start/Stop to resume cooking.
6. When cooking is complete, transfer the rack of lamb to a plate. Serve warm.

Simple Lamb Chops

⏲ PREP TIME: 10 MINUTES, COOK TIME: 15 MINUTES, SERVES 2

- 15 ml olive oil
- 4 (11o g) lamb chops
- Salt and black pepper, to taste

1. Mix the olive oil, salt, and black pepper in a large bowl and add the lamb chops.
2. Install the large grid in drawer 1. Place the chops on the drawer, then insert the drawer in unit.
3. Press Start/Stop button, select Zone 1, select Manual setting, set temperature to 200°C, and set time to 15 minutes. Press Start/Stop button to begin cooking.
4. With 7 minutes remaining, press Start/Stop to pause the unit. Remove the drawer from unit and flip the chops over. Reinsert drawer in unit and press Start/Stop to resume cooking.
5. When cooking is complete, transfer the chops to a plate. Serve warm.

Pesto Coated Rack of Lamb

⏲ PREP TIME: 15 MINUTES, COOK TIME: 18 MINUTES, SERVES 4

- 60 ml extra-virgin olive oil
- 1 (680 g) rack of lamb
- ½ bunch fresh mint
- 1 garlic clove
- 7 ml honey
- Salt and black pepper, to taste

1. Put the olive oil, mint, garlic, honey, salt and black pepper in a blender and pulse until smooth to make pesto.
2. Coat the rack of lamb with this pesto on both sides.
3. Install the large grid in drawer 1. Place the rack of lamb on the drawer, then insert the drawer in unit.
4. Press Start/Stop button, select Zone 1, select Manual setting, set temperature to 200°C, and set time to 18 minutes. Press Start/Stop button to begin cooking.
5. With 8 minutes remaining, press Start/Stop to pause the unit. Remove the drawer from unit and flip the rack of lamb over. Reinsert drawer in unit and press Start/Stop to resume cooking.
6. When cooking is complete, transfer the rack of lamb to a plate and cut the rack into individual ribs to serve.

Chapter 6: LAMB

Italian Lamb Chops with Avocado Mayo

PREP TIME: 5 MINUTES, COOK TIME: 12 MINUTES, SERVES 2

- 2 lamb chops
- 120 ml mayonnaise
- 15 ml lemon juice
- 2 avocados
- 2 tsps. Italian herbs

1. Season the lamb chops with the Italian herbs, then set aside for about 5 minutes.
2. Install the large grid in drawer 1. Place the lamb chops on the drawer, then insert the drawer in unit.
3. Press Start/Stop button, select Zone 1, select Manual setting, set temperature to 200°C, and set time to 12 minutes. Press Start/Stop button to begin cooking.
4. With 6 minutes remaining, press Start/Stop to pause the unit. Remove the drawer from unit and flip the lamb chops over. Reinsert drawer in unit and press Start/Stop to resume cooking.
5. Meanwhile, halve the avocados and open to remove the pits. Spoon the flesh into a blender.
6. Put the mayonnaise and lemon juice and pulse until a smooth consistency is achieved.
7. When cooking is complete, transfer the lamb chops to a plate. Serve warm with the avocado mayo.

....

Lamb Burger

PREP TIME: 15 MINUTES, COOK TIME: 22-23 MINUTES, SERVES 4

- 10 ml olive oil
- 400 g minced lamb
- 70 g black olives, finely chopped
- 40 g crumbled feta cheese
- ⅓ onion, finely chopped
- 1 clove garlic, minced
- 8 g fresh parsley, finely chopped
- 1½ tsps. fresh oregano, finely chopped
- ½ tsp. salt
- freshly ground black pepper
- 4 thick pitta breads
- toppings and condiments

1. Preheat a medium frying pan over medium-high heat on the hob. Add the olive oil and cook the onion until tender, but not browned about 4 to 5 minutes. Add the garlic and cook for another minute. Transfer the onion and garlic to a mixing bowl and add the minced lamb, parsley, oregano, olives, feta cheese, salt and pepper. Gently mix the ingredients together.
2. Divide the lamb mixture into 4 equal portions and then form the hamburgers, being careful not to over-handle the meat. One good way to do this is to throw the meat back and forth between the hands like a baseball, packing the meat each time you catch it. Flatten the balls into patties, making an indentation in the centre of each patty. Flatten the sides of the patties as well to make it easier to fit them into the drawer.
3. Install the large grid in drawer 1. Place the burgers in a single layer on the drawer, then insert the drawer in unit.
4. Press Start/Stop button, select Zone 1, select Manual setting, set temperature to 190°C, and set time to 16 minutes. Press Start/Stop button to begin cooking.
5. With 8 minutes remaining, press Start/Stop to pause the unit. Remove the drawer from unit and flip the burgers over. Reinsert drawer in unit and press Start/Stop to resume cooking.
6. When cooking is complete, transfer burgers to a plate and let the burgers rest for a few minutes before dressing and serving.
7. While the burgers are resting, cook the pittas in the air fryer for 2 minutes. Tuck the burgers into the toasted pittas, or wrap the pittas around the burgers and serve with a tzatziki sauce or some mayonnaise.

....

Fast Lamb Satay

PREP TIME: 5 MINUTES, COOK TIME: 10 MINUTES, SERVES 2

- Cooking spray
- 2 boneless lamb steaks
- 1 tsp. ginger
- ¼ tsp. cumin
- ½ tsp. nutmeg
- Salt and ground black pepper, to taste

1. Combine the cumin, nutmeg, ginger, salt and pepper in a small bowl.
2. Cube the lamb steaks and massage the spice mixture into each one.
3. Leave to marinate for about 10 minutes, then transfer onto metal skewers.
4. Install the large grid in drawer 1. Place the skewers on the drawer and spritz with cooking spray, then insert the drawer in unit.
5. Press Start/Stop button, select Zone 1, select Manual setting, set temperature to 200°C, and set time to 10 minutes. Press Start/Stop button to begin cooking.
6. With 5 minutes remaining, press Start/Stop to pause the unit. Remove the drawer from unit and flip the skewers over. Reinsert drawer in unit and press Start/Stop to resume cooking.
7. When cooking is complete, transfer the skewers to a plate. Serve warm.

Lollipop Lamb Chops

PREP TIME: 15 MINUTES, COOK TIME: 18 MINUTES, SERVES 4

- 120 ml olive oil
- 8 lamb chops (1 rack)
- 45 g shelled pistachios
- 20 g packed fresh mint
- 30 g grated Parmesan cheese
- 15 g packed fresh parsley
- ½ small clove garlic
- 2 ml lemon juice
- ¼ tsp. salt
- 30 ml vegetable oil
- 1 tbsp. dried rosemary, chopped
- 1 tbsp. dried thyme
- Salt and freshly ground black pepper, to taste

1. Make the pesto by combining the garlic, parsley and mint in a food processor and process until finely chopped. Add the Parmesan cheese, lemon juice, pistachios and salt. Process until all the ingredients have turned into a paste. With the processor running, slowly pour the olive oil in. Scrape the sides of the processor with a spatula and process for another 30 seconds.
2. Rub both sides of the lamb chops with vegetable oil and season with salt, black pepper, rosemary and thyme, pressing the herbs into the meat gently with the fingers.
3. Install the grids in drawers. Place 5 lamb chops on the drawer 1 and 3 lamb chops on the drawer 2, then insert the drawers in unit.
4. Press Start/Stop button, select Zone 1, select Manual setting, set temperature to 200°C, and set time to 18 minutes. Select Zone 2 and repeat the settings for Zone 1. Press Start/Stop button to begin cooking.
5. Flip the lamb chops for even cooking and browning halfway through cooking.
6. When cooking is complete, transfer the lamb chops to a plate. Serve the lamb chops with mint pesto drizzled on top.

Scrumptious Lamb Chops

PREP TIME: 20 MINUTES, COOK TIME: 18 MINUTES, SERVES 4

- 45 ml olive oil
- 5 g fresh mint leaves, minced
- 4 (170 g) lamb chops
- 2 carrots, peeled and cubed
- 1 fennel bulb, cubed
- 1 parsnip, peeled and cubed
- 1 garlic clove, minced
- 2 tbsps. dried rosemary
- Salt and black pepper, to taste

1. Mix the herbs, garlic and olive oil in a large bowl and coat the lamb chops generously with this mixture.
2. Marinate in the refrigerator for about 3 hours.
3. Soak the vegetables in a large pan of water for about 15 minutes.
4. Install the grids in drawers. Place the lamb chops on the drawer 1 and vegetables on the drawer 2, then insert the drawers in unit.
5. Press Start/Stop button, select Zone 1, select Manual setting, set temperature to 200°C, and set time to 18 minutes. Select Zone 2, select Vegetables setting, set temperature to 200°C, and set time to 16 minutes. Press SYNC and Start/Stop button to begin cooking.
6. With 8 minutes remaining, press Start/Stop to pause the unit. Remove the drawers from unit and flip the lamb chops and vegetables over. Reinsert drawers in unit and press Start/Stop to resume cooking.
7. When cooking is complete, serve lamb chops with vegetables.

Za'atar Lamb Loin Chops

PREP TIME: 10 MINUTES, COOK TIME: 16 MINUTES, SERVES 4

- 5 ml olive oil
- 8 (100 g) bone-in lamb loin chops, trimmed
- 15 ml fresh lemon juice
- 3 garlic cloves, crushed
- 1 tbsp. Za'atar
- Salt and black pepper, to taste

1. Mix the garlic, lemon juice, oil, Za'atar, salt, and black pepper in a large bowl.
2. Coat the lamb loin chops generously with the herb mixture.
3. Install the grids in drawers. Place 5 chops on the drawer 1 and 3 chops on the drawer 2, then insert the drawers in unit.
4. Press Start/Stop button, select Zone 1, select Manual setting, set temperature to 200°C, and set time to 16 minutes. Select Zone 2 and repeat the settings for Zone 1. Press Start/Stop button to begin cooking.
5. Flip the chops for even cooking and browning halfway through cooking.
6. When cooking is complete, transfer the chops to a plate. Serve warm.

(Note: Za'atar - Za'atar is generally made with ground dried thyme, oregano, marjoram, or some combination thereof, mixed with toasted sesame seeds, and salt, though other spices such as sumac might also be added. Some commercial varieties also include roasted flour.)

CHAPTER 7
Beef

Beef Braising Cheeseburgers ·· 39

Sriracha Beef Short Ribs ·· 39

Tasty Beef Jerky ·· 40

Bacon Wrapped Beef Hot Dog ·· 40

Herbed Beef Loin ·· 41

Buttered Filet Mignon ·· 41

Ribeye Steaks with Rosemary ··· 42

Beef Braising Steak with Brussels Sprouts ································· 42

Roasted Beef with Onion ··· 42

Beef and Veggies ··· 43

Rubbed Rib Steak ·· 43

Perfect Skirt Steak ··· 43

Beef Braising Cheeseburgers

PREP TIME: 10 MINUTES, COOK TIME: 12 MINUTES, SERVES 4

- 350 g beef braising steak, minced
- 4 slices Cheddar cheese
- 4 ciabatta rolls
- 1 envelope onion soup mix
- coarse salt and freshly ground black pepper, to taste
- 1 tsp. paprika

1. In a large bowl, stir together the minced braising steak, onion soup mix, salt, black pepper, and paprika to combine well.
2. Shape the mixture into four equal patties.
3. Install the large grid in drawer 1. Place the patties on the drawer, then insert the drawer in unit.
4. Press Start/Stop button, select Zone 1, select Manual setting, set temperature to 200°C, and set time to 12 minutes. Press Start/Stop button to begin cooking.
5. With 1 minute remaining, press Start/Stop to pause the unit. Remove the drawer from unit and put the slices of cheese on the top of the patties. Reinsert drawer in unit and press Start/Stop to resume cooking.
6. When cooking is complete, transfer the patties to a plate. Serve warm on ciabatta rolls.

Sriracha Beef Short Ribs

PREP TIME: 15 MINUTES, COOK TIME: 20 MINUTES, SERVES 8

- 1.8 kg bone-in beef short ribs
- 240 ml low-sodium soy sauce
- 120 ml rice vinegar
- 80 g spring onions, chopped
- 30 g brown sugar
- 15 ml Sriracha
- 1 tbsp. fresh ginger, finely grated
- 1 tsp. ground black pepper

1. Put the beef short ribs with all other ingredients in a resealable bag and seal the bag.
2. Shake to coat evenly and refrigerate overnight.
3. Install the grids in drawers. Remove the short ribs from resealable bag and arrange the ribs in a single layer on the drawers. Insert the drawers in unit.
4. Press Start/Stop button, select Zone 1, select Manual setting, set temperature to 200°C, and set time to 20 minutes. Select Zone 2 and repeat the settings for Zone 1. Press Start/Stop button to begin cooking.
5. With 10 minutes remaining, press Start/Stop to pause the unit. Remove the drawers from unit and flip the ribs over. Reinsert drawers in unit and press Start/Stop to resume cooking.
6. When cooking is complete, transfer the ribs to a plate. Serve warm.

Bacon Wrapped Beef Hot Dog

PREP TIME: 5 MINUTES, COOK TIME: 12 MINUTES, SERVES 4

- 4 beef hot dogs
- 4 rashers of sugar-free bacon

1. Take a rasher of bacon and wrap it around the hot dog, securing it with a toothpick. Repeat with the other pieces of bacon and hot dogs.
2. Install the large grid in drawer 1. Place the wrapped dogs on the drawer, then insert the drawer in unit.
3. Press Start/Stop button, select Zone 1, select Manual setting, set temperature to 200°C, and set time to 12 minutes. Press Start/Stop button to begin cooking.
4. Flip the wrapped dogs for even cooking and browning halfway through cooking.
5. When cooking is complete, transfer the wrapped dogs to a plate. Serve warm.

Tasty Beef Jerky

PREP TIME: 20 MINUTES, COOK TIME: 5 HOURS, SERVES 3

- 500 g beef silverside, cut into thin strips
- 120 ml soy sauce
- 100 g dark brown sugar
- 60 ml Worcestershire sauce
- 15 ml chilli pepper sauce
- 1 tbsp. hickory liquid smoke
- 1 tsp. cayenne pepper
- 1 tsp. garlic powder
- 1 tsp. onion powder
- ½ tsp. smoked paprika
- ½ tsp. ground black pepper

1. Mix the brown sugar, all sauces, liquid smoke, and spices in a medium bowl.
2. Coat the beef strips with the marinade generously and marinate overnight.
3. Install the grids in drawers. According to the size of the drawers, arrange the beef strips on the drawers reasonably. Insert the drawers in unit.
4. Press Start/Stop button, select Zone 1, select Dehydrate setting, set temperature to 65°C, and set time to 5 hours. Select Zone 2 and repeat the settings for Zone 1. Press Start/Stop button to begin cooking.
5. When cooking is complete, transfer the beef jerky to a plate. Serve warm.

Herbed Beef Loin

PREP TIME: 5 MINUTES, COOK TIME: 15 MINUTES, SERVES 4

- 15 g butter, melted
- 500 g beef loin
- 1 tsp. garlic salt
- ¼ tsp. dried thyme
- ¼ tsp. dried parsley

1. In a small bowl, combine the melted butter, thyme, garlic salt, and parsley.
2. Cut the beef into slices and generously apply the seasoned butter with a brush.
3. Install the large grid in drawer 1. Place the beef on the drawer, then insert the drawer in unit.
4. Press Start/Stop button, select Zone 1, select Manual setting, set temperature to 200°C, and set time to 15 minutes. Press Start/Stop button to begin cooking.
5. Flip the beef slices for even cooking and browning halfway through cooking.
6. When cooking is complete, transfer the beef to a plate. Serve warm.

Buttered Filet Mignon

PREP TIME: 10 MINUTES, COOK TIME: 15 MINUTES, SERVES 4

- 15 g butter, softened
- 2 (170 g) filet mignon steaks
- Salt and black pepper, to taste

1. Rub the filet mignon steaks generously with salt and black pepper and coat with butter.
2. Install the large grid in drawer 1. Place the steaks on the drawer, then insert the drawer in unit.
3. Press Start/Stop button, select Zone 1, select Manual setting, set temperature to 200°C, and set time to 15 minutes. Press Start/Stop button to begin cooking.
4. Flip the steaks for even cooking and browning halfway through cooking.
5. When cooking is complete, transfer the steaks to a plate and cut into desired size slices to serve.

Ribeye Steaks with Rosemary

PREP TIME: 10 MINUTES, COOK TIME: 16 MINUTES, SERVES 2

- 30 g butter
- 2 ribeye steaks
- 20 ml balsamic vinegar
- 5 g rosemary, chopped
- 1 clove garlic, minced
- Salt and ground black pepper, to taste

1. In a frying pan, melt the butter over medium heat. Add the garlic and fry until fragrant.
2. Remove the frying pan from the heat and add the salt, black pepper, and vinegar. Allow it to cool.
3. Add the rosemary, then pour the mixture into a Ziploc bag.
4. Put the ribeye steaks in the bag and shake well, coating the meat well. Refrigerate for an hour, then allow to sit for about 20 minutes.
5. Install the grids in drawers. According to the size of the drawers, arrange the ribeyes on the drawers reasonably. Insert the drawers in unit.
6. Press Start/Stop button, select Zone 1, select Manual setting, set temperature to 200°C, and set time to 16 minutes. Select Zone 2 and repeat the settings for Zone 1. Press Start/Stop button to begin cooking.
7. Flip the ribeyes for even cooking and browning halfway through cooking.
8. When cooking is complete, transfer the ribeyes to a plate. Serve warm.

....

Beef Braising Steak with Brussels Sprouts

PREP TIME: 20 MINUTES, COOK TIME: 25 MINUTES, SERVES 4

- 30 ml vegetable oil
- 500 g beef braising steak
- 15 ml red wine vinegar
- 1 tsp. fine sea salt
- ½ tsp. ground black pepper
- 1 tsp. onion powder
- 1 tsp. smoked paprika
- ½ tsp. garlic powder
- 225 g Brussels sprouts, cleaned and halved
- 1 tsp. dried basil
- 1 tsp. dried sage
- ½ tsp. fennel seeds

1. Massage the beef with the vegetable oil, wine vinegar, paprika, salt, black pepper, onion powder, and garlic powder, coating it well.
2. Allow to marinate for a minimum of 3 hours.
3. Install the grids in drawers. Remove the beef from the marinade and put on the drawer 1. Place Brussels sprouts on the drawer 2 along with the fennel seeds, basil, and sage, then insert the drawers in unit.
4. Press Start/Stop button, select Zone 1, select Manual setting, set temperature to 200°C, and set time to 20 minutes. Select Zone 2, select Brussels sprouts setting, set temperature to 200°C, and set time to 25 minutes. Press SYNC and Start/Stop button to begin cooking.
5. With 10 minutes remaining, press Start/Stop to pause the unit. Remove the drawers from unit. Flip the beef over and shake Brussels sprouts for 10 seconds. Reinsert drawers in unit and press Start/Stop to resume cooking.
6. When cooking is complete, serve beef with Brussels sprouts.

....

Roasted Beef with Onion

PREP TIME: 15 MINUTES, COOK TIME: 18 MINUTES, SERVES 2

- 15 ml avocado oil
- 450 g top round beef, cut into 4-cm cubes
- ½ yellow onion, chopped
- 30 ml Worcestershire sauce
- 1 tsp. onion powder
- 1 tsp. garlic powder
- Salt and black pepper, to taste

1. Mix the beef, onion, Worcestershire sauce, avocado oil, and spices in a bowl.
2. Install the large grid in drawer 1. Place the beef mixture on the drawer, then insert the drawer in unit.
3. Press Start/Stop button, select Zone 1, select Manual setting, set temperature to 200°C, and set time to 18 minutes. Press Start/Stop button to begin cooking.
4. With 18 minutes remaining, press START/PAUSE to pause the unit. Remove the drawer from unit and shake for 10 seconds. Reinsert drawer in unit and press START/PAUSE to resume cooking.
5. When cooking is complete, transfer the beef mixture to a plate and cut into desired size slices to serve.

Beef and Veggies

PREP TIME: 15 MINUTES, COOK TIME: 18 MINUTES, SERVES 4

- **30 ml olive oil**
- **450 g top round steak, cut into cubes**
- **115 g broccoli, cut into florets**
- **115 g mushrooms, sliced**
- **15 ml apple cider vinegar**
- **1 tsp. fine sea salt**
- **1 tsp. shallot powder**
- **1 tsp. dried basil**
- **1 tsp. celery seeds**
- **½ tsp. ground black pepper**
- **¾ tsp. smoked cayenne pepper**
- **½ tsp. garlic powder**
- **¼ tsp. ground cumin**

1. Massage the olive oil, vinegar, shallot powder, cayenne pepper, garlic powder, salt, black pepper, and cumin into the cubed steak, ensuring to coat each piece evenly.
2. Allow to marinate for at least 3 hours.
3. Install the grids in drawers. Place the beef on the drawer 1 and vegetables on the drawer 2, then insert the drawers in unit.
4. Press Start/Stop button, select Zone 1, select Manual setting, set temperature to 200°C, and set time to 14 minutes. Select Zone 2, select Vegetables setting, set temperature to 200°C, and set time to 18 minutes. Press SYNC and Start/Stop button to begin cooking.
5. With 7 minutes remaining, press Start/Stop to pause the unit. Remove the drawers from unit and shake for 10 seconds. Reinsert drawers in unit and press Start/Stop to resume cooking.
6. When cooking is complete, serve the beef with vegetables.

Rubbed Rib Steak

PREP TIME: 10 MINUTES, COOK TIME: 20 MINUTES, SERVES 4

- **15 ml olive oil**
- **900 g rib steak**
- **400 g steak rub**

1. Rub the rib steak generously with steak rub, salt and black pepper, and coat evenly with olive oil.
2. Install the large grid in drawer 1. Place the steak on the drawer, then insert the drawer in unit.
3. Press Start/Stop button, select Zone 1, select Manual setting, set temperature to 200°C, and set time to 20 minutes. Press Start/Stop button to begin cooking.
4. Flip the steak for even cooking and browning halfway through cooking.
5. When cooking is complete, transfer the steak to a plate and cut into desired size slices to serve.

(Note: To prepare the Steak Rub - 2 tbsps. fresh cracked black pepper, 2 tbsps. coarse salt, 2 tbsps. paprika, 1 tbsp. crushed red pepper flakes, 1 tbsp. crushed coriander seeds (not ground), 1 tbsp. garlic powder, 1 tbsp. onion powder, 2 tsps. cayenne pepper. Mix all ingredients in a medium bowl and stir well to combine.)

Perfect Skirt Steak

PREP TIME: 15 MINUTES, COOK TIME: 16 MINUTES, SERVES 4

- **180 ml olive oil**
- **2 (225 g) skirt steaks**
- **45 ml red wine vinegar**
- **60 g fresh parsley leaves, chopped finely**
- **10 g fresh oregano, chopped finely**
- **10 g fresh mint leaves, chopped finely**
- **3 garlic cloves, minced**
- **1 tbsp. ground cumin**
- **2 tsps. smoked paprika**
- **1 tsp. red pepper flakes, crushed**
- **1 tsp. cayenne pepper**
- **Salt and freshly ground black pepper, to taste**

1. Season the skirt steaks with a little salt and black pepper.
2. In a large bowl, mix all the ingredients except the steaks.
3. Put 4 tbsps. herb mixture and steaks in a resealable bag and shake well.
4. Refrigerate for about 24 hours and reserve the remaining herb mixture.
5. Keep the steaks at room temperature for 30 minutes.
6. Install the large grid in drawer 1. Place the steaks on the drawer, then insert the drawer in unit.
7. Press Start/Stop button, select Zone 1, select Manual setting, set temperature to 200°C, and set time to 16 minutes. Press Start/Stop button to begin cooking.
8. With 8 minutes remaining, press Start/Stop to pause the unit. Remove the drawer from unit and flip the steaks over. Reinsert drawer in unit and press Start/Stop to resume cooking.
9. When cooking is complete, transfer the steaks to a plate and sprinkle with remaining herb mixture to serve.

CHAPTER 8

Pork

Mustard Bacon Wrapped Pork Tenderloin 45

Chinese Pork Meatballs with Brussels Sprouts 45

Citrus Pork Loin Roast 46

BBQ Pork Steaks 46

Sweet and Sour Pork Chops 47

Classic Scotch Eggs 47

Garlic Pork Chops 48

Cornflour Pork Spare Ribs 48

Breaded Pork Chops and Parsnips 48

Cheese Crusted Pork Chops 49

Bacon Wrapped Jalapeño Poppers 49

Crunchy Pork Chops 49

Mustard Bacon Wrapped Pork Tenderloin

PREP TIME: 15 MINUTES, COOK TIME: 30 MINUTES, SERVES 4

- 4 rashers of bacon
- 1 (700 g) pork tenderloin
- 30 g Dijon mustard

1. Rub the pork tenderloin evenly with mustard and wrap the tenderloin with rashers of bacon.
2. Install the large grid in drawer 1. Place the pork tenderloin on the drawer, then insert the drawer in unit.
3. Press Start/Stop button, select Zone 1, select Manual setting, set temperature to 190°C, and set time to 30 minutes. Press Start/Stop button to begin cooking.
4. With 15 minutes remaining, press Start/Stop to pause the unit. Remove the drawer from unit and flip the pork tenderloin over. Reinsert drawer in unit and press Start/Stop to resume cooking.
5. When cooking is complete, transfer the pork tenderloin to a plate. Cut into desired size slices to serve.

Chinese Pork Meatballs with Brussels Sprouts

PREP TIME: 15 MINUTES, COOK TIME: 22 MINUTES, SERVES 3

- For the Meatballs:
- 7 ml olive oil
- 170 g minced pork
- 1 egg, beaten
- 30 g cornflour
- 7 ml light soy sauce
- 5 ml oyster sauce
- 2 ml sesame oil
- ¼ tsp. five spice powder
- ¼ tsp. honey
- For the Brussels Sprouts:
- 300 g Brussels sprouts, trimmed and halved lengthwise
- 15 ml maple syrup
- 15 ml balsamic vinegar
- Salt, as required

1. Mix all the ingredients for Brussels Sprouts in a medium bowl and toss to coat well.
2. Mix all the ingredients for the meatballs in a small bowl except cornflour and oil until well combined.
3. Shape the pork mixture into equal-sized balls and place the cornflour in a shallow dish.
4. Roll the meatballs evenly into cornflour mixture.
5. Install the grids in drawers. Place Brussels Sprouts on the drawer 1 and meatballs on the drawer 2, then insert the drawers in unit.
6. Press Start/Stop button, select Zone 1, select Vegetables setting, set temperature to 200°C, and set time to 22 minutes. Select Zone 2, select Manual setting, set temperature to 190°C, and set time to 16 minutes. Press SYNC and Start/Stop button to begin cooking.
7. With 8 minutes remaining, press Start/Stop to pause the unit. Remove the drawers from unit and shake the Brussels Sprouts and meatballs for 10 seconds. Reinsert drawers in unit and press Start/Stop to resume cooking.
8. When cooking is complete, serve the meatballs with Brussels Sprouts.

Chapter 8: PORK

BBQ Pork Steaks

PREP TIME: 5 MINUTES, COOK TIME: 17 MINUTES, SERVES 4

- 4 pork steaks
- 100 g brown sugar
- 120 ml ketchup
- 30 ml BBQ sauce
- 15 g Cajun seasoning
- 15 ml vinegar
- 5 ml soy sauce

1. Sprinkle the pork steaks with Cajun seasoning.
2. Combine the remaining ingredients and brush onto the steaks.
3. Install the grids in drawers. Place 3 steaks on the drawer 1 and 1 steak on the drawer 2, then insert the drawers in unit.
4. Press Start/Stop button, select Zone 1, select Manual setting, set temperature to 190°C, and set time to 17 minutes. Select Zone 2 and repeat the settings for Zone 1. Press Start/Stop button to begin cooking.
5. With 8 minutes remaining, press Start/Stop to pause the unit. Remove the drawers from unit and flip the steaks over. Reinsert drawers in unit and press Start/Stop to resume cooking.
6. When cooking is complete, transfer the steaks to a plate. Serve warm.

Citrus Pork Loin Roast

PREP TIME: 10 MINUTES, COOK TIME: 40 MINUTES, SERVES 8

- **Cooking spray**
- **900 g boneless pork loin roast**
- 20 g orange marmalade
- 15 ml lime juice
- 1 tsp. coarse brown mustard
- 1 tsp. curry powder
- 1 tsp. dried lemongrass
- **Salt and ground black pepper, to taste**

1. Mix the marmalade, lime juice, mustard, curry powder, and lemongrass.
2. Rub the pork mixture all over the surface of the pork loin. Season with salt and pepper.
3. Install the large grid in drawer 1. Place the pork roast diagonally on the drawer, then insert the drawer in unit.
4. Press Start/Stop button, select Zone 1, select Manual setting, set temperature to 190°C, and set time to 40 minutes. Press Start/Stop button to begin cooking.
5. With 20 minutes remaining, press Start/Stop to pause the unit. Remove the drawer from unit and flip the pork roast. Reinsert drawer in unit and press Start/Stop to resume cooking.
6. When cooking is complete, wrap roast in foil and let rest for 10 minutes before slicing.

Chapter 8: PORK

Sweet and Sour Pork Chops

PREP TIME: 10 MINUTES, COOK TIME: 20 MINUTES, SERVES 4

- 4 pork loin chops
- 2 garlic cloves, minced
- 30 ml soy sauce
- 30 ml honey
- 15 ml balsamic vinegar
- ¼ tsp. ground ginger
- Salt and black pepper, to taste

1. Season the pork loin chops with a little salt and black pepper.
2. Mix the remaining ingredients in a large bowl and add the chops.
3. Coat with the marinade generously and cover to refrigerate for about 8 hours.
4. Install the grids in drawers. Place 3 chops on the drawer 1 and 1 chop on the drawer 2, then insert the drawers in unit.
5. Press Start/Stop button, select Zone 1, select Manual setting, set temperature to 190°C, and set time to 20 minutes. Select Zone 2 and repeat the settings for Zone 1. Press Start/Stop button to begin cooking.
6. With 10 minutes remaining, press Start/Stop to pause the unit. Remove the drawers from unit and flip the chops over. Reinsert drawers in unit and press Start/Stop to resume cooking.
7. When cooking is complete, transfer the chops to a plate. Serve warm.

Classic Scotch Eggs

PREP TIME: 5 MINUTES, COOK TIME: 17 MINUTES, MAKES 4 EGGS

- Cooking spray
- 500 g Mexican chorizo or other seasoned sausage meat
- 4 soft-boiled eggs plus 1 raw egg
- 100 g panko bread crumbs
- 50 g plain flour
- 15 ml water

1. Divide the Mexican chorizo into 4 equal portions. Flatten each portion into a disc. Place a soft-boiled egg in the centre of each disc. Wrap the chorizo around the egg, encasing it completely. Place the encased eggs on a plate and chill for at least 30 minutes.
2. Beat the raw egg with 15 ml water. Place the flour on a small plate and the panko on a second plate. Working with 1 egg at a time, roll the encased egg in the flour, then dip it in the egg mixture. Dredge the egg in the panko and place on a plate. Repeat with the remaining eggs.
3. Install the large grid in drawer 1. Spray the eggs with oil and place on the drawer, then insert the drawer in unit.
4. Press Start/Stop button, select Zone 1, select Manual setting, set temperature to 200°C, and set time to 17 minutes. Press Start/Stop button to begin cooking.
5. With 8 minutes remaining, press Start/Stop to pause the unit. Remove the drawer from unit and flip the eggs over. Reinsert drawer in unit and press Start/Stop to resume cooking.
6. When cooking is complete, transfer the eggs to a plate. Serve warm.

Garlic Pork Chops

PREP TIME: 10 MINUTES, COOK TIME: 20 MINUTES, SERVES 4

- 15 ml coconut oil
- 4 pork chops
- 15 g coconut butter
- 2 tsps. garlic, grated
- 2 g parsley
- Salt and black pepper, to taste

1. Mix all the seasonings, coconut oil, garlic, butter, and parsley in a bowl and coat the pork chops with it.
2. Cover the pork chops with foil and refrigerate to marinate for about 1 hour.
3. Install the grids in drawers. Remove the foil, arrange 3 chops on the drawer 1 and 1 chop on the drawer 2, then insert the drawers in unit.
4. Press Start/Stop button, select Zone 1, select Manual setting, set temperature to 190°C, and set time to 20 minutes. Select Zone 2 and repeat the settings for Zone 1. Press Start/Stop button to begin cooking.
5. With 10 minutes remaining, press Start/Stop to pause the unit. Remove the drawers from unit and flip the chops over. Reinsert drawers in unit and press Start/Stop to resume cooking.
6. When cooking is complete, transfer the pork chops to a plate. Serve warm.

Cornflour Pork Spare Ribs

PREP TIME: 15 MINUTES, COOK TIME: 22 MINUTES, SERVES 6

- 30 ml olive oil
- 12 (2.5-cm) pork spare ribs
- 5-6 garlic cloves, minced
- 120 ml rice vinegar
- 60 g cornflour
- 30 ml soy sauce
- Salt and black pepper, to taste

1. Mix the garlic, soy sauce, vinegar, salt, and black pepper in a large bowl.
2. Coat the pork spare ribs generously with the garlic mixture and refrigerate to marinate overnight.
3. Place the cornflour in a shallow bowl and dredge the ribs in it. Drizzle with olive oil.
4. Install the grids in drawers. According to the size of the drawers, arrange the ribs on the drawers reasonably. Insert the drawers in unit.
5. Press Start/Stop button, select Zone 1, select Manual setting, set temperature to 190°C, and set time to 22 minutes. Select Zone 2 and repeat the settings for Zone 1. Press Start/Stop button to begin cooking.
6. With 10 minutes remaining, press Start/Stop to pause the unit. Remove the drawers from unit and flip the ribs over. Reinsert drawers in unit and press Start/Stop to resume cooking.
7. When cooking is complete, transfer the ribs to a plate. Serve warm.

Breaded Pork Chops and Parsnips

PREP TIME: 15 MINUTES, COOK TIME: 30 MINUTES, SERVES 2

- 15 g butter, melted
- 15 ml vegetable oil
- 300 g parsnips, peeled and cut into 2.5 cm chunks
- 2 (170 g) pork chops
- 1 egg
- 115 g breadcrumbs
- 30 g plain flour
- Salt and black pepper, to taste

1. Mix the parsnips and butter in a bowl and toss to coat well.
2. Season the pork chops with salt and black pepper.
3. Place the flour in a shallow bowl and whisk an egg in a second bowl.
4. Mix the breadcrumbs and vegetable oil in a third bowl.
5. Coat the pork chops with flour, dip into egg and dredge into the breadcrumb mixture.
6. Install the grids in drawers. Place chops on the drawer 1 and parsnips on the drawer 2, then insert the drawers in unit.
7. Press Start/Stop button, select Zone 1, select Manual setting, set temperature to 190°C, and set time to 18 minutes. Select Zone 2, select Vegetables setting, set temperature to 200°C, and set time to 30 minutes. Press SYNC and Start/Stop button to begin cooking.
8. With 10 minutes remaining, press Start/Stop to pause the unit. Remove the drawers from unit. Flip the chops over and shake the parsnips for 10 seconds. Reinsert drawers in unit and press Start/Stop to resume cooking.
9. When cooking is complete, serve the chops with parsnips.

Chapter 8: PORK

Cheese Crusted Pork Chops

PREP TIME: 10 MINUTES, COOK TIME: 18 MINUTES, SERVES 5

- Cooking spray
- 5 thick boneless pork chops
- 2 beaten eggs
- 80 g pork rind crumbs
- 30 g grated Parmesan cheese
- ¼ tsp. black pepper
- ½ tsp. salt
- ¼ tsp. chilli powder
- ½ tsp. onion powder
- 1 tsp. smoked paprika

1. Rub the black pepper and salt on both sides of pork chops.
2. In a food processor, pulse the pork rinds into crumbs. Mix the crumbs with chilli powder, onion powder, and paprika in a bowl.
3. Beat the eggs in another bowl.
4. Dip the pork chops into the eggs then into pork rind crumb mixture.
5. Install the grids in drawers. Place 3 pork chops on the drawer 1 and 2 pork chops on the drawer 2, then insert the drawers in unit.
6. Press Start/Stop button, select Zone 1, select Manual setting, set temperature to 190°C, and set time to 18 minutes. Select Zone 2 and repeat the settings for Zone 1. Press Start/Stop button to begin cooking.
7. With 9 minutes remaining, press Start/Stop to pause the unit. Remove the drawers from unit and flip the pork chops over. Reinsert drawers in unit and press Start/Stop to resume cooking.
8. When cooking is complete, transfer the pork chops to a plate. Serve warm.

Bacon Wrapped Jalapeño Poppers

PREP TIME: 5 MINUTES, COOK TIME: 16 MINUTES, SERVES 6

- 6 large jalapeños
- 6 rashers of middle bacon, halved
- 110 g ⅓-less-fat cream cheese
- 30 g shredded reduced-fat sharp Cheddar cheese
- 2 spring onions, green tops only, sliced

1. Wearing rubber gloves, halve the jalapeños lengthwise to make 12 pieces. Scoop out the seeds and membranes and discard.
2. In a medium bowl, combine the cream cheese, Cheddar cheese, and spring onions. Using a small spoon, fill the jalapeños with the cream cheese filling. Wrap a rasher of bacon around each pepper and secure with a toothpick.
3. Install the grids in drawers. According to the size of the drawers, arrange the stuffed peppers in a single layer on the drawers reasonably. Insert the drawers in unit.
4. Press Start/Stop button, select Zone 1, select Manual setting, set temperature to 200°C, and set time to 16 minutes. Select Zone 2 and repeat the settings for Zone 1. Press Start/Stop button to begin cooking, until the peppers are tender, the bacon is browned and crisp, and the cheese is melted.
5. When cooking is complete, transfer the stuffed peppers to a plate. Serve warm.

Crunchy Pork Chops

PREP TIME: 15 MINUTES, COOK TIME: 16 MINUTES, SERVES 2

- 1 oil mister
- 2 pork chops
- 90 g xanthum gum
- 1 egg white
- ½ tsp. sea salt
- ¼ tsp. freshly ground black pepper

1. Whisk the egg white with salt and black pepper in a bowl and dip the pork chops in it.
2. Cover the bowl and marinate for about 20 minutes.
3. Pour the xanthum gum over both sides of the pork chops and spray with oil mister.
4. Install the large grid in drawer 1. Place the chops on the drawer, then insert the drawer in unit.
5. Press Start/Stop button, select Zone 1, select Manual setting, set temperature to 190°C, and set time to 16 minutes. Press Start/Stop button to begin cooking.
6. Flip the chops for even cooking and browning halfway through cooking.
7. When cooking is complete, transfer the chops to a plate. Serve warm.

CHAPTER 9
Snack

Garlic Matchstick Fries 51

Crispy Banana Chips 51

Homemade Mozzarella Arancini 52

Rosemary Baked Cashews 52

Yummy Strawberry Slices 53

Easy Tortilla Crisps 53

Crispy Pot Stickers 54

Prosciutto Wrapped Asparagus 54

Coconut-Crusted Prawn 54

Spiced Sweet Potato Chips 55

Dehydrated Kiwi Fruit 55

Air Fried Green Olives 55

Garlic Matchstick Fries

PREP TIME: 5 MINUTES, COOK TIME: 18 MINUTES, SERVES 2

- 15 ml vegetable oil
- 1 large russet potato (about 340 g), scrubbed clean, and julienned
- 1 garlic clove, thinly sliced
- Leaves from 1 sprig fresh rosemary
- Coarse salt and freshly ground black pepper, to taste
- Flaky sea salt, for serving

1. Place the julienned potatoes in a large colander and rinse under cold running water until the water runs clear. Spread the potatoes out on a double-thick layer of paper towels and pat dry.
2. In a large bowl, combine the potatoes, oil, and rosemary. Season with coarse salt and pepper and toss to coat evenly.
3. Install the large grid in drawer 1. Place the julienned potato on the drawer, then insert the drawer in unit.
4. Press Start/Stop button, select Zone 1, select Fries setting, set temperature to 200°C, and set time to 18 minutes. Press Start/Stop button to begin cooking.
5. Shake the fries for even cooking and browning halfway through cooking.
6. When cooking is complete, transfer the fries to a plate and sprinkle with flaky sea salt while they're hot. Serve immediately.

Crispy Banana Chips

PREP TIME: 10 MINUTES, COOK TIME: 7 HOURS, SERVES: 4

- spray bottle of lemon juice
- 2 medium bananas, peeled and cut across into 3-mm-thick slices

1. Lightly spray the banana slices with lemon juice.
2. Install the grids in drawers. According to the size of the drawers, arrange the banana slices on the drawers reasonably. Insert the drawers in unit.
3. Press Start/Stop button, select Zone 1, select Dehydrate setting, set temperature to 40°C, and set time to 7 hours. Select Zone 2 and repeat the settings for Zone 1. Press Start/Stop button to begin cooking.
4. When cooking is complete, transfer the banana chips to a plate. Serve immediately.

Chapter 9: SNACK / 51

Rosemary Baked Cashews

PREP TIME: 5 MINUTES, COOK TIME: 5 MINUTES, SERVES 4

- Cooking spray
- 5 ml olive oil
- 300 g roasted and unsalted whole cashews
- 2 sprigs of fresh rosemary (1 chopped and 1 whole)
- 2 ml honey
- 1 tsp. coarse salt

1. In a medium bowl, whisk together the olive oil, chopped rosemary, coarse salt, and honey. Set aside.
2. Install the large grid in drawer 1 and spray with cooking spray. Place the cashews and the whole rosemary sprig on the drawer, then insert the drawer in unit.
3. Press Start/Stop button, select Zone 1, select Manual setting, set temperature to 150°C, and set time to 5 minutes. Press Start/Stop button to begin cooking.
4. When cooking is complete, discard the rosemary and transfer the cashews to the olive oil mixture, tossing to coat evenly.
5. Allow to cool for about 15 minutes before serving.

Homemade Mozzarella Arancini

PREP TIME: 5 MINUTES, COOK TIME: 12 MINUTES, MAKES 16 ARANCINI

- 30 ml olive oil
- 400 g cooked rice, cooled
- 2 eggs, beaten
- 16 (2-cm) cubes Mozzarella cheese
- 180 g panko bread crumbs, divided
- 50 g grated Parmesan cheese
- 4 g minced fresh basil

1. In a medium bowl, combine the cooked rice, eggs, 60 g bread crumbs, Parmesan cheese, and basil. Form this mixture into 16 (4-cm) balls.
2. Poke a hole in each of the balls with your finger and insert a Mozzarella cube. Form the rice mixture firmly around the cheese.
3. On a shallow plate, combine the remaining 120 g bread crumbs with the olive oil and mix well. Roll the balls in the bread crumbs to coat evenly.
4. Install the grids in drawers. Place 10 balls on the drawer 1 and 6 balls on the drawer 2, then insert the drawers in unit.
5. Press Start/Stop button, select Zone 1, select Manual setting, set temperature to 180°C, and set time to 12 minutes. Select Zone 2 and repeat the settings for Zone 1. Press Start/Stop button to begin cooking, until golden brown.
6. When cooking is complete, serve hot.

Yummy Strawberry Slices

PREP TIME: 20 MINUTES, **COOK TIME:** 7 HOURS, **SERVES:** 4

- spray bottle of lemon juice
- 300 g strawberries, washed and hulled, then thin sliced

1. Lightly spray the strawberry slices with lemon juice.
2. Install the grids in drawers. According to the size of the drawers, arrange the strawberry slices on the drawers reasonably. Insert the drawers in unit.
3. Press Start/Stop button, select Zone 1, select Dehydrate setting, set temperature to 40°C, and set time to 7 hours. Select Zone 2 and repeat the settings for Zone 1. Press Start/Stop button to begin cooking.
4. When cooking is complete, transfer the strawberry slices to a plate. Serve immediately.

Easy Tortilla Crisps

PREP TIME: 5 MINUTES, **COOK TIME:** 5 MINUTES, **SERVES** 2

- 15 ml olive oil
- 8 corn tortillas
- Salt, to taste

1. Slice the corn tortillas into triangles. Brush lightly with olive oil.
2. Install the grids in drawers. According to the size of the drawers, arrange the tortilla pieces on the drawers reasonably. Insert the drawers in unit.
3. Press Start/Stop button, select Zone 1, select Manual setting, set temperature to 200°C, and set time to 5 minutes. Select Zone 2 and repeat the settings for Zone 1. Press Start/Stop button to begin cooking.
4. When cooking is complete, transfer the tortilla pieces to a plate. Season with salt before serving.

Chapter 8: PORK / 53

Crispy Pot Stickers

PREP TIME: 10 MINUTES, COOK TIME: 12 MINUTES, MAKES 30 POT STICKERS

- 1 egg, beaten
- 30 wonton wrappers
- 50 g finely chopped cabbage
- 30 g finely chopped red bell pepper
- 2 spring onions, finely chopped
- 30 ml cocktail sauce
- 10 ml low-sodium soy sauce
- 15 ml water, for brushing the wrappers

1. In a small bowl, combine the cabbage, red pepper, egg, spring onions, cocktail sauce, and soy sauce, and mix well.
2. Put about 1 tsp. of the mixture in the centre of each wonton wrapper. Fold the wrapper in half, covering the filling; dampen the edges with water, and seal. You can crimp the edges of the wrapper with your fingers so they look like the pot stickers you get in restaurants. Brush them with water.
3. Install the grids in drawers. According to the size of the drawers, arrange the pot stickers on the drawers reasonably. Insert the drawers in unit.
4. Press Start/Stop button, select Zone 1, select Manual setting, set temperature to 180°C, and set time to 12 minutes. Select Zone 2 and repeat the settings for Zone 1. Press Start/Stop button to begin cooking, until the pot stickers are hot and the bottoms are lightly browned.
5. When cooking is complete, serve hot.

Prosciutto Wrapped Asparagus

PREP TIME: 5 MINUTES, COOK TIME: 12 MINUTES, SERVES 6

- Cooking spray
- 12 asparagus spears, woody ends trimmed
- 24 pieces thinly sliced prosciutto

1. Wrap each asparagus with 2 slices of prosciutto, then repeat this process with the remaining asparagus and prosciutto.
2. Install the grids in drawers. According to the size of the drawers, arrange the asparagus bundles on the drawers reasonably. Insert the drawers in unit.
3. Press Start/Stop button, select Zone 1, select Vegetables setting, set temperature to 200°C, and set time to 12 minutes. Select Zone 2 and repeat the settings for Zone 1. Press Start/Stop button to begin cooking.
4. With 6 minutes remaining, press Start/Stop to pause the unit. Remove the drawers from unit and flip the bundles. Reinsert drawers in unit and press Start/Stop to resume cooking.
5. When cooking is complete, remove the bundles and allow to cool on a wire rack for about 5 minutes before serving.

Coconut-Crusted Prawn

PREP TIME: 10 MINUTES, COOK TIME: 7 MINUTES, SERVES 2 TO 4

- Cooking spray
- 225 g medium prawns, peeled and deveined (tails intact)
- 240 ml tinned coconut milk
- 50 g panko bread crumbs
- 50 g unsweetened desiccated coconut
- Finely grated zest of 1 lime
- Coarse salt, to taste
- Freshly ground black pepper, to taste
- 1 small or ½ medium cucumber, halved and deseeded
- 240 ml coconut yoghurt
- 1 jalapeno pepper, deseeded and minced

1. In a bowl, combine the prawns, coconut milk, lime zest, and ½ tsp. coarse salt. Let the prawns stand for about 10 minutes.
2. Meanwhile, in a separate bowl, stir together the bread crumbs and desiccated coconut and season with salt and pepper.
3. A few at a time, add the prawns to the bread crumb mixture and toss to coat completely. Transfer the prawns to a wire rack set over a baking sheet. Spray the prawn all over with cooking spray.
4. Install the large grid in drawer 1. Place the prawns on the drawer, then insert the drawer in unit.
5. Press Start/Stop button, select Zone 1, select Fish setting, set temperature to 200°C, and set time to 7 minutes. Press Start/Stop button to begin cooking.
6. Flip the prawns for even cooking and browning halfway through cooking.
7. When cooking is complete, transfer the prawns to a serving platter and season with more salt.
8. Grate the cucumber into a small bowl. Stir in the coconut yoghurt and jalapeno pepper and season with salt and black pepper. Serve alongside the prawns while they're warm.

Spiced Sweet Potato Chips

PREP TIME: 10 MINUTES, COOK TIME: 25 MINUTES, SERVES 2

- 30 ml olive oil
- 2 medium sweet potatoes (about 280 g each), cut into wedges, 1-cm thick and 7-cm long
- 1½ tsps. smoked paprika
- 1½ tsps. coarse salt, plus more as needed
- 1 tsp. chilli powder
- ½ tsp. ground turmeric
- ½ tsp. ground cumin
- ½ tsp. mustard powder
- ¼ tsp. cayenne pepper
- 160 ml sour cream
- 1 garlic clove, grated
- Freshly ground black pepper, to taste

1. In a large bowl, combine the olive oil, paprika, chilli powder, cumin, turmeric, mustard powder, salt, and cayenne. Add the sweet potatoes, season with black pepper, and toss to coat evenly.
2. Install the large grid in drawer 1. Place the sweet potato wedges on the drawer, then insert the drawer in unit.
3. Press Start/Stop button, select Zone 1, select Fries setting, set temperature to 200°C, and set time to 25 minutes. Press Start/Stop button to begin cooking.
4. Shake the sweet potato wedges for even cooking and browning halfway through cooking.
5. Meanwhile, stir together the sour cream and garlic in a small bowl. Season with salt and black pepper and transfer to a serving dish.
6. When cooking is complete, return the potato wedges to the reserved bowl and toss again while they are hot.
7. Serve the potato wedges hot with the garlic sour cream.

Dehydrated Kiwi Fruit

PREP TIME: 20 MINUTES, COOK TIME: 8 HOURS, SERVES:3

- spray bottle of lemon juice
- 3 medium kiwi fruits, peeled and sliced as thinly as you can

1. Lightly spray the kiwi slices with lemon juice.
2. Install the grids in drawers. According to the size of the drawers, arrange the kiwi slices on the drawers reasonably. Insert the drawers in unit.
3. Press Start/Stop button, select Zone 1, select Dehydrate setting, set temperature to 40°C, and set time to 8 hours. Select Zone 2 and repeat the settings for Zone 1. Press Start/Stop button to begin cooking.
4. When cooking is complete, transfer the kiwi slices to a plate. Serve immediately.

Air Fried Green Olives

PREP TIME: 5 MINUTES, COOK TIME: 8 MINUTES, SERVES 4

- Cooking spray
- 1 (160 g) jar pitted green olives
- 1 egg
- 50 g plain flour
- 50 g bread crumbs
- Salt and pepper, to taste

1. Remove the green olives from the jar and dry thoroughly with paper towels.
2. In a small bowl, combine the flour with salt and black pepper to taste. Place the bread crumbs in another small bowl. In a third small bowl, beat the egg.
3. Dip the green olives in the flour, then the egg, and then the bread crumbs.
4. Install the large grid in drawer 1 and spritz with cooking spray. Place the breaded olives on the drawer, then insert the drawer in unit.
5. Press Start/Stop button, select Zone 1, select Manual setting, set temperature to 200°C, and set time to 8 minutes. Press Start/Stop button to begin cooking.
6. Shake the olives for even cooking and browning halfway through cooking.
7. When cooking is complete, transfer the olives to a plate. Cool before serving.

CHAPTER 10
Dessert

Simple Apple Tart ·· 57

Flavour-Packed Clafoutis ·· 57

Tasty Lava Cake ··· 58

Healthy Sunflower Seeds Bread ··· 58

Homemade Buttermilk Scones ·· 59

Classic Pecan Pie ··· 59

Garlic Bread Rolls ··· 60

Cinnamon Bread Pudding ··· 60

Peach Parcel ·· 60

Fast Chocolate Balls ·· 61

Chocolate Coconut Brownies ··· 61

Simple Pineapple Sticks ··· 61

Simple Apple Tart

PREP TIME: 15 MINUTES, COOK TIME: 25 MINUTES, SERVES 2

- 70 g butter, chopped and divided
- 1 large apple, peeled, cored and cut into 12 wedges
- 100 g flour
- 1 egg yolk
- 30 g sugar

1. Grease a 18x13 cm baking pan lightly.
2. Mix half of the butter and flour in a bowl until a soft dough is formed.
3. Roll the dough into 15-cm round on a floured surface.
4. Place the remaining butter and sugar into the baking pan and arrange the apple wedges in a circular pattern.
5. Top with rolled dough and press gently along the edges of the pan.
6. Install the large grid in drawer 1. Place the baking pan on the drawer, then insert the drawer in unit.
7. Press Start/Stop button, select Zone 1, select Dessert setting, set temperature to 200°C, and set time to 25 minutes. Press Start/Stop button to begin cooking.
8. When cooking is complete, remove drawer from unit. Serve warm.

Flavour-Packed Clafoutis

PREP TIME: 10 MINUTES, COOK TIME: 30 MINUTES, SERVES 4

- 15 g butter
- 220 g fresh cherries, pitted
- 1 egg
- 30 g flour
- 120 ml sour cream
- 30 g icing sugar
- 45 ml vodka
- 30 g sugar
- Pinch of salt

1. Grease a 18x13 cm baking pan lightly.
2. Mix the cherries and vodka in a bowl.
3. Sift together flour, sugar and salt in another bowl.
4. Stir in the sour cream and egg until a smooth dough is formed.
5. Transfer the dough into the baking pan and top with the cherry mixture and butter.
6. Install the large grid in drawer 1. Place the baking pan on the drawer, then insert the drawer in unit.
7. Press Start/Stop button, select Zone 1, select Dessert setting, set temperature to 160°C, and set time to 30 minutes. Press Start/Stop button to begin cooking.
8. When cooking is complete, dust with icing sugar and serve warm.

Chapter 10: DESSERT / 57

Healthy Sunflower Seeds Bread

PREP TIME: 15 MINUTES, COOK TIME: 18 MINUTES, SERVES 4

- 85 g whole wheat flour
- 85 g plain flour
- 45 g sunflower seeds
- 240 ml lukewarm water
- ½ sachet instant yeast
- 1 tsp. salt

1. Grease a 18x10 cm cake pan.
2. Mix together flours, sunflower seeds, yeast and salt in a large bowl.
3. Add the water slowly and knead for about 5 minutes until a dough is formed.
4. Cover the dough with a clingfilm and keep in warm place for about half an hour.
5. Arrange the dough into the cake pan.
6. Install the large grid in drawer 1. Place the cake pan on the drawer, then insert the drawer in unit.
7. Press Start/Stop button, select Zone 1, select Dessert setting, set temperature to 200°C, and set time to 18 minutes. Press Start/Stop button to begin cooking.
8. When cooking is complete, let the bread cool for 10 minutes and serve warm.

Tasty Lava Cake

PREP TIME: 10 MINUTES, COOK TIME: 6 MINUTES, SERVES 3

- 150 g unsalted butter
- 2 eggs
- 150 g chocolate chips, melted
- 80 g plain flour
- 65 g sugar
- 30 g fresh raspberries
- Salt, to taste

1. Grease three 7-cm ramekins lightly.
2. Mix the sugar, butter, eggs, flour and salt in a bowl until well combined.
3. Fold in the melted chocolate chips and evenly divide this mixture into the prepared ramekins.
4. Install the grids in drawers. Place 2 ramekins on the drawer 1 and 1 ramekin on the drawer 2, then insert the drawers in unit.
5. Press Start/Stop button, select Zone 1, select Dessert setting, set temperature to 180°C, and set time to 6 minutes. Select Zone 2 and repeat the settings for Zone 1. Press Start/Stop button to begin cooking.
6. When cooking is complete, let the cakes cool slightly. Garnish with raspberries and serve immediately.

Chapter 10: DESSERT

Homemade Buttermilk Scones

⏱ PREP TIME: 15 MINUTES, COOK TIME: 8 MINUTES, SERVES 4

- 75 g unsalted butter, cut into cubes
- 200 g plain flour
- 180 ml buttermilk
- 4 g baking soda
- 3 g baking powder
- 4 g granulated sugar
- Salt, to taste

1. Grease a 13-cm pie dish lightly.
2. Sift together flour, baking soda, baking powder, sugar and salt in a large bowl.
3. Add the cold butter and mix until a coarse crumb is formed.
4. Stir in the buttermilk gently and mix until a dough is formed.
5. Press the dough into 1-cm thickness onto a floured surface and cut out circles with a 4-cm round cookie cutter.
6. Arrange the scones in the pie dish in a single layer and brush with butter.
7. Install the large grid in drawer 1. Place the pie dish on the drawer, then insert the drawer in unit.
8. Press Start/Stop button, select Zone 1, select Dessert setting, set temperature to 200°C, and set time to 8 minutes. Press Start/Stop button to begin cooking.
9. When cooking is complete, let the scones cool sightly and serve warm.

Classic Pecan Pie

⏱ PREP TIME: 10 MINUTES, COOK TIME: 35 MINUTES, SERVES 6

- 75 g butter, melted
- 1 frozen pie crust, thawed
- 100 g pecan halves
- 2 large eggs
- 150 g brown sugar
- 50 g caster sugar
- 15 g flour
- 1 tsp. vanilla extract

1. Grease a 13-cm pie dish lightly.
2. Mix both sugars, eggs and butter in a large bowl until smooth.
3. Stir in the milk flour, and vanilla extract and beat until well combined.
4. Fold in the pecan halves and arrange the crust in the bottom of pie dish. Put the pecan mixture in pie crust evenly.
5. Install the large grid in drawer 1. Place the pie dish on the drawer, then insert the drawer in unit.
6. Press Start/Stop button, select Zone 1, select Dessert setting, set temperature to 150°C, and set time to 35 minutes. Press Start/Stop button to begin cooking.
7. When cooking is complete, let the pie cool slightly and serve warm.

Garlic Bread Rolls

PREP TIME: 10 MINUTES, COOK TIME: 6 MINUTES, SERVES 2

- Cooking spray
- 30 g unsalted butter, melted
- 2 bread rolls
- 60 g Parmesan cheese, grated
- ½ tsp. garlic bread seasoning mix

1. Cut the bread rolls in slits and stuff the cheese in the slits.
2. Top with the butter and garlic bread seasoning mix.
3. Install the large grid in drawer 1 and spray with cooking spray. Place the bread rolls on the drawer, then insert the drawer in unit.
4. Press Start/Stop button, select Zone 1, select Dessert setting, set temperature to 180°C, and set time to 6 minutes. Press Start/Stop button to begin cooking.
5. With 3 minutes remaining, press Start/Stop to pause the unit. Remove the drawer from unit and flip the bread rolls over. Reinsert drawer in unit and press Start/Stop to resume cooking.
6. When cooking is complete, transfer the bread rolls to a plate. Serve warm.

....

Cinnamon Bread Pudding

PREP TIME: 10 MINUTES, COOK TIME: 12 MINUTES, SERVES 2

- 2 bread slices, cut into small cubes
- 1 egg
- 240 ml milk
- 30 g sultanas, soaked in hot water for about 15 minutes
- 15 g chocolate chips
- 15 g sugar
- 12 g brown sugar
- ½ tsp. ground cinnamon
- ¼ tsp. vanilla extract

1. Grease a 18x13 cm baking dish lightly.
2. Mix the egg, milk, brown sugar, cinnamon and vanilla extract until well combined.
3. Stir in the sultanas and combine well.
4. Arrange the bread cubes evenly in the baking dish and top with the milk mixture.
5. Refrigerate for 20 minutes and sprinkle with chocolate chips and sugar.
6. Install the large grid in drawer 1. Place the baking dish on the drawer, then insert the drawer in unit.
7. Press Start/Stop button, select Zone 1, select Dessert setting, set temperature to 190°C, and set time to 12 minutes. Press Start/Stop button to begin cooking.
8. When cooking is complete, transfer the bread pudding to a plate. Serve warm.

....

Peach Parcel

PREP TIME: 10 MINUTES, COOK TIME: 15 MINUTES, SERVES 2

- 2 puff pastry sheets
- 1 peach, peeled, cored and halved
- 240 ml prepared vanilla custard
- 1 egg, beaten lightly
- 15 g sugar
- 15 ml whipped cream
- Pinch of ground cinnamon

1. Place a spoonful of vanilla custard and a peach half in the centre of each pastry sheet.
2. Mix the sugar and cinnamon in a small bowl and sprinkle on the peach halves.
3. Pinch the corners of sheets together to shape into a parcel.
4. Install the large grid in drawer 1. Place the parcels on the drawer, then insert the drawer in unit.
5. Press Start/Stop button, select Zone 1, select Dessert setting, set temperature to 170°C, and set time to 15 minutes. Press Start/Stop button to begin cooking.
6. When cooking is complete, remove drawer from unit. Top the parcels with whipped cream. Transfer to a plate and serve with remaining custard.

Fast Chocolate Balls

PREP TIME: 15 MINUTES, COOK TIME: 13 MINUTES, SERVES 8

- cooking spray
- 250 g plain flour
- 170 g chilled butter
- 15 g cocoa powder
- 60 g icing sugar
- 45 g chocolate, chopped into 8 chunks
- 1 tsp. vanilla extract
- Pinch of ground cinnamon

1. Mix the flour, icing sugar, cocoa powder, cinnamon and vanilla extract in a bowl.
2. Add the cold butter and buttermilk and mix until a smooth dough is formed.
3. Divide the dough into 8 equal balls and press 1 chocolate chunk in the centre of each ball. Cover completely with the dough.
4. Install the grids in drawers. Place 5 balls on the drawer 1 and 3 balls on the drawer 2, then insert the drawers in unit.
5. Press Start/Stop button, select Zone 1, select Dessert setting, set temperature to 180°C, and set time to 13 minutes. Select Zone 2 and repeat the settings for Zone 1. Press Start/Stop button to begin cooking.
6. With 5 minutes remaining, press Start/Stop to pause the unit. Set the Air fryer to 160°C and press Start/Stop to resume cooking.
7. When cooking is complete, transfer the balls to a plate. Serve warm.

Chocolate Coconut Brownies

PREP TIME: 15 MINUTES, COOK TIME: 15 MINUTES, SERVES 8

- 120 ml coconut oil
- 4 whisked eggs
- 60 g dark chocolate
- 200 g sugar
- 60 g flour
- 60 g desiccated coconut
- 37 ml water
- 15 ml honey
- ¼ tsp. ground cinnamon
- ½ tsp. ground star anise
- ¼ tsp. coconut extract
- ½ tsp. vanilla extract
- Sugar, for dusting

1. Melt the coconut oil and dark chocolate in the microwave.
2. Combine with the eggs, cinnamon, sugar, water, anise, coconut extract, vanilla, and honey in a large bowl.
3. Stir in the flour and desiccated coconut. Incorporate everything well.
4. Lightly grease a 18x13 cm baking dish with butter. Transfer the mixture to the dish.
5. Install the large grid in drawer 1. Place the baking dish on the drawer, then insert the drawer in unit.
6. Press Start/Stop button, select Zone 1, select Dessert setting, set temperature to 180°C, and set time to 15 minutes. Press Start/Stop button to begin cooking.
7. When cooking is complete, let the brownies cool slightly. Take care when taking it out of the baking dish. Slice it into squares. Dust with sugar before serving.

Simple Pineapple Sticks

PREP TIME: 5 MINUTES, COOK TIME: 10 MINUTES, SERVES 4

- ½ fresh pineapple, cut into sticks
- 20 g desiccated coconut

1. Coat the pineapple sticks in the desiccated coconut.
2. Install the large grid in drawer 1. Place the pineapple sticks on the drawer, then insert the drawer in unit.
3. Press Start/Stop button, select Zone 1, select Manual setting, set temperature to 200°C, and set time to 10 minutes. Press Start/Stop button to begin cooking.
4. Flip the pineapple sticks for even cooking and browning halfway through cooking.
5. When cooking is complete, transfer the pineapple sticks to a plate. Serve warm.

APPENDIX 1: TEFAL DUAL ZONE AIR FRYER TIMETABLE

The table below helps you to select the basic settings for the food you want to prepare. Note: The cooking times below are only a guide and may vary according to the variety and batch of potatoes used. For other food the size, shape and brand may affect results. Therefore, you may need to adjust the cooking time slightly.

Ingredient	Quantity		Time	Temp	Mode	Tip
Potatoes & Fries						
Frozen fries (10 mm x 10 mm standard thickness)	Drawer 1	600-1400 g	25-40 min	180°C	FRIES	
	Drawer 2	300-800 g	25-35 min			
Homemade fries (8 mm x 8 mm)	Drawer 1	500 g	40 min	180°C	FRIES	Dry it by towel before cooking
	Drawer 2	200 g	35 min			
Frozen potato wedges	Drawer 1	600-1400 g	25-40 min	180°C	FRIES	
	Drawer 2	300-800 g	25-40 min			
Meat & Poultry						
Frozen beef burgers	Drawer 1	up to 4 pieces	10-18 min	200°C	MANUAL	
	Drawer 2	up to 2 pieces	10-15 min			
Chicken breast fillets (boneless)	Drawer 1	up to 4 pieces	10 min	200°C	CHICKEN	
	Drawer 2	up to 2 pieces	10 min			
Chicken whole	Drawer 1	up to 1300 g	50 min	160°C	CHICKEN	Drawer 1 only
Snacks						
Chicken nuggets	Drawer 1	up to 1 kg	12 min	200°C	CHICKEN	
	Drawer 2	up to 400 g	12 min			
Chicken wings	Drawer 1	up to 1 kg or 8/9 pieces	22 min	200°C	CHICKEN	
	Drawer 2	up to 400 g or 4/5 pieces	22 min			
Pizza	Drawer 1	up to 3 slices	5 min	170°C	MANUAL	
	Drawer 2	up to 2 slices	5 min			
Vegetables	Drawer 1	up to 1 kg	20 min	200°C	VEGETABLES	
	Drawer 2	400-600 g	20 min			
Fish						
Salmon fillet	Drawer 1	up to 4 pieces	8-10 min	200°C	FISH	
	Drawer 2	up to 2 pieces	8-10 min			
Prawns	Drawer 1	up to 500 g to 1 kg	8-10 min	200°C	FISH	
	Drawer 2	up to 400 g	8-10 min			
Baking						
Muffins	Drawer 1	up to 6/8 pieces	16 min	160°C	DESSERT	
	Drawer 2	up to 4 pieces	16 min			
Chocolate cakes	Drawer 1	1 round cake pan	30-35 min	160°C	DESSERT	
Dehydrate						
Sliced Apple	Drawer 1	8 slices	8h	40°C	DEHYDRATE	
	Drawer 2	4 slices	8h			

GRILL PROGRAM* (depending on model)

Ingredient	Type of cooking		Quantity	Time	Temp	Tip
Beef	Drawer 1	rare	up to 4 pieces	4 min	200°C	Drawer 1 only. You can add oil, aromatic herbs and salt for better taste. At midcooking, you can return the food.
		medium	up to 4 pieces	6 min	200°C	
		well-done	up to 4 pieces	8 min	200°C	
Pork chops	Drawer 1	done	up to 3 pieces	12-16 min	200°C	
Lamb loin chops	Drawer 1	done	up to 4-6 pieces	12-14 min	200°C	
Chicken fillets	Drawer 1	done	up to 4-6 pieces	10 min	200°C	
Sausages	Drawer 1	done	up to 8-10 pieces	16-20 min	200°C	
Fish fillets	Drawer 1	done	up to 4-6 pieces	8 min	200°C	

APPENDIX 2: MEASUREMENT CONVERSION CHART

WEIGHT EQUIVALENTS

METRIC	US STANDARD	US STANDARD (OUNCES)
15 g	1 tablespoon	1/2 ounce
30 g	1/8 cup	1 ounce
60 g	1/4 cup	2 ounces
115 g	1/2 cup	4 ounces
170 g	3/4 cup	6 ounces
225 g	1 cup	8 ounces
450 g	2 cups	16 ounces
900 g	4 cups	2 pounds

VOLUME EQUIVALENTS

METRIC	US STANDARD	US STANDARD (OUNCES)
15 ml	1 tablespoon	1/2 fl.oz.
30 ml	2 tablespoons	1 fl.oz.
60 ml	1/4 cup	2 fl.oz.
125 ml	1/2 cup	4 fl.oz.
180 ml	3/4 cup	6 fl.oz.
250 ml	1 cup	8 fl.oz.
500 ml	2 cups	16 fl.oz.
1000 ml	4 cups	1 quart

TEMPERATURES EQUIVALENTS

CELSIUS (C)	FAHRENHEIT (F) (APPROXIMATE)
120 °C	250 °F
135 °C	275 °F
150 °C	300 °F
160 °C	325 °F
175 °C	350 °F
190 °C	375 °F
205 °C	400 °F
220 °C	425 °F
230 °C	450 °F
245 °C	475 °F
260 °C	500 °F

LENGTH EQUIVALENTS

METRIC	IMPERIAL
3 mm	1/8 inch
6 mm	1/4 inch
1 cm	1/2 inch
2.5 cm	1 inch
3 cm	1 1/4 inches
5 cm	2 inches
10 cm	4 inches
15 cm	6 inches
20 cm	8 inches

APPENDIX 3: RECIPES INDEX

A

APPLE
Nutty Apple Muffins	11
Simple Apple Tart	57

ASPARAGUS
Roasted Asparagus with Grated Parmesan	23
Prosciutto Wrapped Asparagus	54

AUBERGINE
Dehydrated Aubergine Slices	24
Spices Stuffed Aubergines	25

AVOCADO
Gold Avocado Fries	10

B

BANANA
Crispy Banana Chips	51

BEEF BRAISING STEAK
Beef Braising Cheeseburgers	39
Beef Braising Steak with Brussels Sprouts	42

BEEF HOT DOG
Bacon Wrapped Beef Hot Dog	40

BEEF LOIN
Herbed Beef Loin	41

BEEF SHORT RIB
Sriracha Beef Short Ribs	39

BEEF SILVERSIDE
Tasty Beef Jerky	40

BLUEBERRY
Quick Blueberry Muffins	9

BROCCOLI
Broccoli with Cauliflower	24

BRUSSELS SPROUTS
Caramelised Brussels Sprouts	22

BUTTON MUSHROOM
Feta Mushroom Frittata	11
Cheese Stuffed Mushrooms	25

C

CABBAGE
Crispy Pot Stickers	54

CARROT
Glazed Carrots	23

CASHEW
Rosemary Baked Cashews	52

CHERRY
Flavour-Packed Clafoutis	57

CHICKEN BREAST
Bacon Wrapped Chicken Breasts	15
Chicken with Veggies	18
Roasted Chicken Breasts with Broccoli	19

CHICKEN DRUMSTICK
Chinese Chicken Drumsticks	17
Juicy Chicken Drumsticks	18

CHICKEN TENDER
Flavoury Chicken Kebabs	19

CHICKEN THIGH
Sweet and Sour Chicken Thighs	17

CHICKEN WING
Glazed Chicken Wings	16
Crunchy Chicken Wings	18

CHOCOLATE
Fast Chocolate Balls	61

CHOCOLATE CHIP
Tasty Lava Cake	58

CHORIZO
Classic Scotch Eggs	47

COD

Sweet and Sour Glazed Cod 28
Cod with Asparagus 29
Chilli Cod Cakes 31

D

DARK CHOCOLATE
Chocolate Coconut Brownies 61

F

FILET MIGNON STEAK
Buttered Filet Mignon 41
FLOUNDER
Crispy Flounder with Green Beans 27

G

GREEN BEAN
Green Beans and Mushroom 22
Buttered Green Beans 25
GREEN OLIVE
Air Fried Green Olives 55

H

HADDOCK
Herbed Haddock with Cheese Sauce 31
HALIBUT
Panko Halibut Strips 31

J-K

JALAPEÑO
Bacon Wrapped Jalapeño Poppers 49

KIWI
Dehydrated Kiwi Fruit 55

L

LAMB
Lamb with Potatoes 34
Lamb Meatballs with Tomato Sauce 33
Lamb Burger 36
LAMB CHOP
Simple Lamb Chops 35
Italian Lamb Chops with Avocado Mayo 36
Lollipop Lamb Chops 37
Scrumptious Lamb Chops 37
LAMB LEG
Fantastic Lamb Leg 33
LAMB LOIN CHOP
Za'atar Lamb Loin Chops 37
LAMB RACK
Pesto Coated Rack of Lamb 35
LAMB RIB RACK
Greek Lamb Rack 34
LAMB STEAK
Fast Lamb Satay 36

M

MUSHROOM
Roasted Mushrooms 24

P

PEACH
Peach Parcel 60
Classic Pecan Pie 59
PEPPERONI
Pitta and Pepperoni Pizza 12

PINEAPPLE
Simple Pineapple Sticks	61

PINK SALMON
Simple Salmon Bites	30

PORK
Mustard Pork Meatballs	12
Chinese Pork Meatballs with Brussels Sprouts	45

PORK CHOP
Garlic Pork Chops	48
Breaded Pork Chops and Parsnips	48
Cheese Crusted Pork Chops	49
Crunchy Pork Chops	49

PORK LOIN
Citrus Pork Loin Roast	46

PORK LOIN CHOP
Sweet and Sour Pork Chops	47

PORK SPARE RIB
Cornflour Pork Spare Ribs	48

PORK STEAK
BBQ Pork Steaks	46

PORK TENDERLOIN
Mustard Bacon Wrapped Pork Tenderloin	45

POTATO
Kale and Potato Nuggets	12
Classic British Breakfast	13
Classic Hasselback Potatoes	21
Garlic Matchstick Fries	51

PRAWN
Garlic Prawns	28
Coconut-Crusted Prawn	54

R

RED BELL PEPPER
Mini Red Pepper Cups	21

RIB STEAK
Rubbed Rib Steak	43

RIBEYE STEAK
Ribeye Steaks with Rosemary	42

S

SALMON
Cajun Salmon	30

SCALLOP
Buttered Scallops	27

SKIRT STEAK
Perfect Skirt Steak	43

SPINACH
Feta Spinach Omelette	13

STRAWBERRY
Yummy Strawberry Slices	53

SULTANA
Cinnamon Bread Pudding	60

SUNFLOWER SEED
Healthy Sunflower Seeds Bread	58

SWEET POTATO
Spiced Sweet Potato Chips	55

T

TIGER PRAWN
Paprika Prawns and Brussels Sprouts	30

TILAPIA
Lemon Tilapia	29

TOP ROUND BEEF
Roasted Beef with Onion	42

TOP ROUND STEAK
Beef and Veggies	43

TURKEY
Asian Turkey Meatballs	16

TURKEY BREAST
Mouthwatering Turkey Roll	19

W

WHOLE CHICKEN
Roasted Chicken with Potatoes	15

Dear Friends,

Are you finding meal planning to be a challenging task, unsure of how to effectively utilize the ingredients in your refrigerator? If so, fret not! I'm here to offer you a personalized solution. As a cookbook author, I understand the complexities of meal planning and am excited to introduce a unique approach tailored just for you. With the assistance of ChatGPT, a cutting-edge AI technology, I can provide you with a private and customized four-week meal plan that aligns perfectly with your preferences and needs. All you need to do is provide me with some specific information such as your gender, age, height, any existing health concerns, dietary preferences, and the cooking tools available in your kitchen. With these details, I can create a personalized plan that aligns perfectly with your lifestyle and goals. Don't hesitate to reach out, and let's embark on this culinary journey together!

Warm regards

Contact Email: Healthrecipegroup@outlook.com

Printed in Great Britain
by Amazon